WHO P⸱
IN THE WYCH
ELM?

Volume 1: The Crime Scene Revisited

ALEX MERRILL

With

PETE MERRILL

APS PUBLICATIONS

Who Put Bella In The Wych Elm?

Bella facial reconstruction by Liverpool John Moores University ©2017 Pete Merrill and APS Publications
Front cover: Rik Rawlings (www.rikawlings.co.uk)
Illustrations: Rik Rawlings & Pete Merrill
Other mages reproduced by kind permission of the Library of Birmingham Archives & Collections (LBAC), and West Mercia Police and Worcestershire Archive and Archaeology Service (WAAS).
Research: Ann Swaby www.militaryandfamilyresearch.co.uk

APS Publications,
4 Oakleigh Road, Stourbridge, West Midlands, DY8 2JX
www.andrewsparke.com

Contents

1. 'Shake the Kaleidoscope'~ 1
2. The Discovery ~ 4
3. Hagley Wood ~ 9
4. The Tree ~ 12
5. Professor Webster ~ 21
6. Dr John Lund ~ 29
7. The Birmingham Forensic Laboratory ~ 31
8. At the Crime Scene ~ 35
9. Bodies in Small Places ~ 48
10. The Shoes ~ 52
11. The Clothing and Hair ~ 57
12. The Bones ~ 65
13. Facial Reconstruction ~ 80
14. The Origins of Bella ~ 84
15. Looking Forward ~ 89

Acknowledgements and Freedom of Information (FOI) requests ~ 91
Reference books/media ~ 93
Documents:
Document 1 ~ 94
Statement: Professor Webster, 23rd April, 1943
Document 2 ~ 101
Statement: Dr John Lund - Staff Biologist, 23rd April, 1943
Document 3 ~ 104
Minutes of No.9 Regional Conference 3rd May, 1943
Document 4 ~ 110
Closure Report DCI Nicholls 13th July, 2005

1
'Shake the kaleidoscope'

My journey started on a warm summer's evening in 2017 when I walked to the top of Wychbury Hill, which is situated to the north of the A456 Birmingham to Kidderminster Road in Hagley, on the West Midlands and Worcestershire border.

At the top of the hill stands an eighty-four-foot obelisk which was built in 1747 and which was to be my journey's end. The reason for my walk was not so much to view the obelisk close up or even the fun of climbing the hill, but instead to see the graffiti daubed on its base referencing an unsolved World War Two murder. It had been featured in a newspaper article promoting an up-and-coming documentary on the subject. The mystery fascinated me.

The central narrative for the murder is a well-rehearsed story. Four boys came across the skeletal remains of a woman in the hollow of a tree in Hagley Wood in 1943. Professor Webster—Director of the Birmingham Forensic Laboratory— attended the crime scene to examine the remains. After he provided the investigation with a description of the victim, her clothing and a likely time of death, the parameters for the police investigation were set.

The inquiry followed several different avenues which have been widely reported; all, that is, except for the crime scene itself. Often briefly referenced by different versions, it isn't afforded the same critical analysis as the graffiti, war-time German espionage, a murdered gypsy or prostitute, ritual murder, witchcraft, devil worship and psychic investigators.

In 2005, sixty-two years later, the victim was still left unidentified, the crime unsolved, and the principal exhibits missing, as was also true of some case files. The West Mercia

Constabulary conducted a review, re-examined all the evidence on file, and decided there were no clear investigative leads to be pursued and they closed the case.

My walk to view the graffiti at the obelisk did not lessen my interest; instead, it enticed me to visit the tree. This quest was not easy. If you dig a little below the surface—reading more than one account—you quickly discover three different locations for the tree, as well as various accounts of what happened at the crime scene, which boy found the remains, what they did, and when. Most accounts also come with a touch of artistic creativity and celebrity magic, although critically there are very few source references. This means that the mystery has evolved unchallenged, initially in the minds of newspaper readers and radio listeners, before progressing to television viewers, and then followers of the internet. What was left unexamined, I suspect, was something far removed from, and less glamorous than, the local legends.

As I wanted to pinpoint the 'real' location of the tree, I found myself researching the crime scene. I quickly discovered related documents in addition to artefacts which had not been discussed or published previously. Sorting fact from fiction was complicated further by the disappearance of several things. Not only had the skeletal remains vanished, but all the other exhibits recovered from the crime scene, as well as the laboratory case file relating to *Bella's* discovery.

What I found most interesting was being unable to find any challenge to the initial investigation's parameters—parameters which were born from the three-day examination of exhibits recovered from the crime scene. Professor Webster's reports appear to have been accepted by the police and historians as being factual, rather than an informed opinion offered at the time. All this made me question whether there was another version of the crime scene story to be told.

What if the woman's body had not been placed in the tree soon after death, but she had been killed earlier and her remains hidden in the tree?

Had the police and scientists misinterpreted the scientific findings of the remains and clothing? Had they been biased because of the early investigative findings on the shoes, and had they subsequently made assumptions to support the notion that the murder took place in 1941?

Lastly, West Mercia's closure report referred to the crime scene under the heading 'Forensic Strategy'. They referenced the use of the expertise of a Forensic Archaeologist, a Forensic Anthropologist, a Forensic Environmentalist, a Palaeontologist and an Odontologist; and their consideration of advances in DNA techniques was also noted. They concluded that there was nothing more that could be done at that stage.

I wished to explore if there have been any forensic developments since that decision was made, that could now aid in solving the crime. I know that offering a different version of events will be challenging, controversial and will leave me open to the possibility of ridicule. After all, the case has now been under the microscope for seventy-four years. The police have explored all possible leads and closed the case, indicating that contributions like mine potentially fall into the category of obsessive and theoretical. But in this volume, I want to add a new perspective to the initial phase of the investigation—to shed light on other possibilities, so that others can develop my findings further and eventually identify *Bella*. After all, I am only a fifteen-year-old school boy, not an investigative journalist: what can I possibly offer of value other than an inquisitive, questioning mind and a desire to 'shake the kaleidoscope'?

2
The Discovery

In the 1950s, the official statements relating to those people involved in the discovery of the crime scene and the search of the surrounding area went missing. This means that the version of events I present is my collective view derived from the remaining case files, archive documents, different authors' accounts, newspaper articles, and radio and TV interviews. With different versions of the event being offered, weighing the accuracy of each contribution has been difficult. I have attempted to consider and respect each contribution, providing references to aid the reader in making an informed decision based on the accuracy of my findings.

On Sunday 18th April, 1943, four boys from Lye and Wollescote were out walking the local Clent and Walton Hills, going about their familiar weekend routine. Tommy Willetts[1] was aged seventeen, Bob Farmer and Robert Hart were both aged fifteen, and the youngest, Fred Payne, was aged fourteen. The boys had

---

[1] Tommy is often mis-identified as being the youngest member of the group.

their Lurchers with them in the hopes of catching rabbits to supplement their wartime rations.

Near the end of the day, they were heading home, away from Clent, along the then unnamed Hagley Wood Lane. Upon reaching Hagley Wood, they ventured inside. Bob Farmer[2] spotted a Blackbird leaving an old coppiced elm tree, and went to investigate. Discovering a nest with four eggs, he directed Robert Hart to look at another tree nearby.

Amongst the branches, Hart spotted a semi- enclosed cavity or hollow within the tree. Looking inside, he saw what he thought was an animal skull, and called the other boys over to investigate.

With the base of the hollow measuring approximately three and a half feet, the skull was just out of arm's reach. Bob Farmer decided to break a stick off to help fish it out. He was eventually able to push the stick into the oval hole at the base of the skull (known as the foramen magnum) and extract it from the hollow.

Farmer believes that during this process of "jabbing" at the skull, he shoved some cloth into the foramen magnum. Once extracted, the boys realised it was a human skull and that their discovery was a serious matter. Farmer carefully placed it back into the hollow and they left the scene in a hurry, heading home.[3]

On the outskirts of Wollescote, near the site of Oldnal Pits[4] (which had been closed in 1941), they met seventeen-year-old Donald Payne, Fred's older brother. They told Donald about their discovery and they returned to the tree to show him what they had found, once again hooking the skull out. Farmer also recalls that in the hollow he saw a green bottle, a pair of shoes and more bones. At this point, and fearful of being prosecuted

---

[2] 'Crimestalker Casebook' TV interview 1994.
[3] Express & Star 29th April, 1943 – Stourbridge Inquest.
[4] http://www.blackcountrymuse.com/myths.htm.

for trespassing, they decided to replace the skull again, return home and tell no one what they had found.

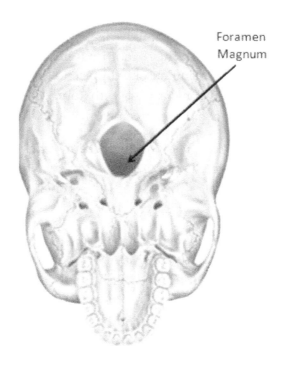

Foramen Magnum

The secret did not last long; Tommy Willetts told his father Harold, who went straight to Lye Police Station, informing Sergeant Charles 'Chris' Lambourne of the find. It was too late to venture out there and then, and it was agreed that they would investigate further in the morning.

The next day, Sergeant Lambourne, along with Tommy Willets,[5] went to Hagley Wood where they met with Sergeant Richard Skerratt from Clent, Constable Jack Pound from Hagley, and the local Motor Patrol Sergeant, Jack Wheeler.

Once Sergeant Skerratt was convinced it was a human skull, he made his way back to Clent Police House, where he phoned the Divisional H.Q. in Stourbridge to report the incident. They, in turn, passed the message onto the County C.I.D, at Hindlip Hall.

---

[5] Some accounts have all the boys returning to the scene.

PC Richard Skerratt c.1936.

It was now late afternoon, and it would take at least twenty-four hours to get all the resources needed to Hagley Wood so it was agreed that Detective Inspector Tom Williams would visit the scene to make an initial assessment and then the crime scene would be guarded until the next day when investigators would conduct a complete examination.

Volunteers were sought and a Special Constable named Douglas Osborne guarded the tree and its contents overnight.

Early afternoon the following day, Tuesday 20th April, Detective Inspector Williams, Sergeant Skerratt and Constable Pound reconvened at the crime scene. They were joined by Detective Superintendent Sidney Inight and the Director of the Birmingham Forensic laboratory, a pathologist Professor James Webster.

3
Hagley Wood

Hagley Wood is located on the A456, midway between Hagley and Halesowen, three and a half miles west of junction 3 of the M5 motorway. The wood lies within parkland which has been part of the Lyttelton family estate (also known as Viscount Cobham's lands) since the 1700s.

In 1943, it was known locally as 'Bluebell Wood'.[6] It was popular with picnickers and lovers, and also served as a playground for children, as it was less dense than the nearby Uffmoor Wood, and Lord Cobham was relatively tolerant towards trespassers.

The Birmingham Blitz and wartime rationing saw an increase in activity in and around the wood. People collected fallen branches for firewood, foraged for berries, nuts and mushrooms, and also partook in poaching, to supplement their official rations. The surrounding roads and lanes also became overnight lay-bys for people from the West Bromwich and Smethwick areas[7] who were escaping the Birmingham bombing.

Today, Hagley Wood occupies the same broad geographical footprint as it did in 1940s. However, there have been a few minor but significant topological changes. The building of the A456 westbound carriageway shaved approximately 100 feet off the northern boundary. The wood was (and still is) prominently made-up of deciduous trees, except for an area of coniferous woodland in the south-east corner, adjacent to Hagley Wood Lane.[8] This area was overplanted many years ago, although there is still evidence of its former boundary.

---

[6] Wolverhampton Express and Star, 7/08/1944.
[7] Police Report No84-17, 29/04/1943, Body Found.
[8] Ordinance Survey Maps, 1903 & 1924.

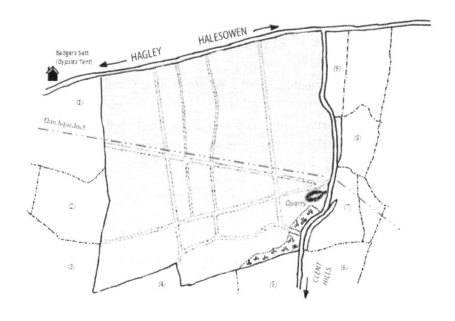

Hagley Wood c. 1940s.

Another relevant change is to the 1940s field layout on the eastern side of the wood. The southern boundary (field eight) has increased. The plot now contains residential and commercial water treatment buildings, including the pump house for the Elan aqueduct.

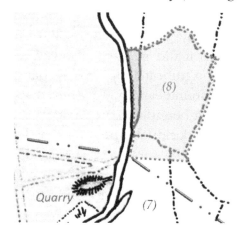

Hagley Wood eastern boundary, field changes.

Added to this, in 1943, the forestry rights—*to cut the trees and purchase the timber* - were under sole contract to J.T Willetts &

Son.[9] They operated from a timber yard located immediately opposite the Rose and Crown Public House in Hasbury.

---

[9] CID Report dated 4th August, 1944, Hagley Road Murder, Chalked Writing on wall and fence at Belle Vale, Halesowen.

4
The Tree

The location and type of tree has also been the subject of conjecture. The official documentation identified the species of tree as Elm, although different accounts have claimed that it was a Hazel tree.

Whilst both have similar leaves, the presence of numerous hazelnut husks in the base of the hollow and the growth pattern of coppiced hazel would lean towards the tree being a Hazel, or *Corylus avellana*.

In any event the tree had been subject to an ancient form of woodland management called coppicing.

This involves the repeated cutting away at a tree stump or stool close to the ground. This action results in the growth of new

shoots; the growth depends on the tree species from the stool or, as in the case of the Hazel, it depends on the ground around the base of the stool. This repeated redressing of a tree causes hollows to develop as the cutting back gets higher.

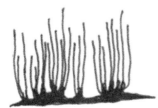

This type of forestry was very popular because it produced fast-growing and sustainable timber without the need to re-plant a tree.

A coppiced tree is a great survivor; it develops an effective root system and thrives from being cut back. Such trees tend to live longer than similar ones which are allowed to grow naturally.

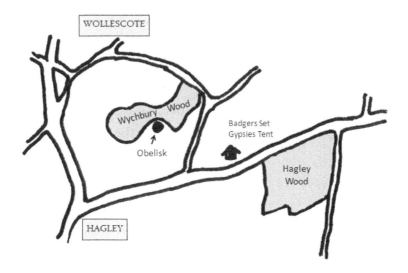

There are several possible locations for the tree, as referenced in different publications,[10] TV shows and documentaries. One is not even in Hagley Wood, but in Wychbury Wood, near the obelisk on Wychbury Hill. This location came about due, initially, to the TV show 'Crimestalker Casebook', which aired in August 1994.[11] Stalker referenced the location as being in Hagley Wood, although he filmed his show in Wychbury Wood, and even used a hollowed-out ancient Yew tree as the main prop.

[10] J M Coley p.20-21, Pl Newman p78, A Sparke p3, D McCormick p.60.
[11] Crimestalker Casebook Bella (14.09.1994) Carlton TV, broadcasted by Central Broadcasting Birmingham.

In September 2005, credibility was added to this location by Midlands TV's 'Inside Out' show, which also filmed in the same location[12]. However, the Yew tree had by then been vandalised, cut down and set alight.

There are three areas identified within Hagley Wood itself as shown on the map on the next page.

The most referenced is [A], 125 yards along Hagley Wood Lane from the Birmingham Road and 25 yards into the woods.[13]

In 2017, Jayne Harris' documentary[14] put the location as [B], approximately 1000 feet down Hagley Wood Lane,[15] and visible at the time 100 yards (300 feet) inside the wood.

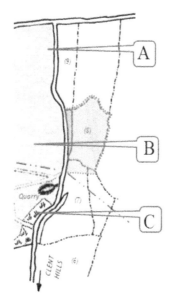

The official report,[16] and evidence given at the inquest[17] by Sergeant Skerratt, indicate another location [C]. He reports, "...that the wood in which the body was found was thick with undergrowth and that the tree was 35 to 40 paces inside the wood from a narrow lane, and the main Birmingham to Kidderminster Road was 630 yards away."

This creates several possibilities for the location of the tree, depending on how Sergeant Skerratt made his calculations. A pace could mean either one normal walking step—two and a half feet—or a double step, sometimes also known as a 'surveyor's pace',

---

[12] Identified by Richard Reichbach, a retired Hagley Estate Manager.

[13] First reported in the Express and Star 22nd April, 1943.

[14] J Harris (2017) The Untold Secrets, identified by an unnamed former Hagley Hall Groundsman.

[15] Field (7) was used as a camping/caravan site.

[16] Minutes of No.9 Regional Police Conference, 3rd May, 1943.

[17] Express & Star 29th April, 1943 – Stourbridge Inquest.

where one starts and ends on the same foot, covering a distance of five feet.

The distance from the Birmingham to Kidderminster Road was reported as being 630 yards. This measurement could be a direct line of sight, or along the route of the lane, which today is known as Hagley Wood Lane.

	Distance in	
	Walking Steps	Surveyor's Pace
35-40 paces	87 ½ - 100 feet	175 – 200 feet

Location [C] is also reported elsewhere. However, the tree is used as the orientation point, with the reader expected to have knowledge of its location. This, combined with only loose references to topographical features, offers several possibilities within [C].

Part of the inquiry focused on the Smiths[18] and Butlers - two Gypsy families who spent Christmas 1942 in Nimmings Field (plot 5), and were described as being camped "about 120 yards from the tree in which the remains were found"; whilst their exact location in the field is not known, the distance would indicate area [C]. Within this part of the inquiry, a witness[19] also makes reference to "a very nasty smell at a point in the bend in the lane 40 to 50 yards above the Birmingham water track (Elan aqueduct) where the skeleton was found". Unfortunately, although the witness was sure it was before the discovery, she was unable to recall when it was exactly.

---

[18] Report Superintendent TN Williams, 05/10/1949.
[19] Statement Mrs PM Tate, taken by Sergeant Skerrett, 28/09/1949.

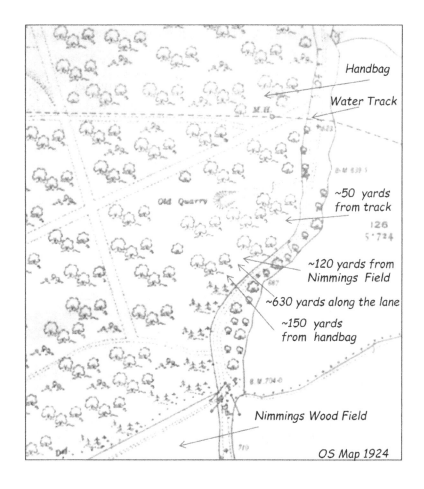

Handbag

Water Track

~50 yards
from track

~120 yards from
Nimmings Field

~630 yards along the lane

~150 yards
from handbag

Nimmings Wood Field

OS Map 1924

Another reference[20] relates to when Special Constable R Sheppard (Hagley Section) found a handbag in Hagley Wood on 17th November, 1944. The following day PC Pound recovered the handbag and recalls "that the handbag was at the base of a Birch tree, which was located in relation to the Wych Elm tree approximately 170 yards to the north side, and was about 20 yards to the north of the Birmingham Water Works 'Ride' (Elan aqueduct) and 25 to 30 yards west of Hagley Wood Lane." It was later identified as belonging to a Dr Dorothy Markham, having been stolen from her car on 16th December, 1939 when it was parked on Hagley Wood Lane.

---

[20] PC 302 Pound memorandum's 20/11 & 23/11/1944; Lady's handbag in wood.

These reference points all converge on the southeast corner of Hagley Wood, in an area between the old quarry and the coniferous wooded northern boundary, and on the bend within the midway section of the 'chicane' in the lane.

The mixture of different scales of measurement—yards, feet, inches and paces—probably contributed to the contradiction in locations. The direction taken by the boys and Sergeant Skerrett into the crime scene was from Clent. It is therefore likely that the measurements for location [A] were the distance measurements from their (Clent) perspectives, and the 'from the road' perspective was added. 125 yards from the Clent direction is similar to the distance from Nimmings Wood Field.

There are two images of the tree in popular circulation; the most widely used graphic contains an arrow indicating that the 'body was found here'. The picture was published in the Express and Star on Friday 20th November, 1953.

The melodramatic article was entitled, *Night visit to Hagley wood... ...and the ghoulish tree coffin - The conclusions I reach on the facts.*

The author was Lieutenant Colonel Wilfred Byford-Jones, a regular contributor to the Wolverhampton Express and Star under the penname 'Quaestor Seeker'. It was this article that resulted in the correspondence from 'Anna of Claverley' which claimed that Bella had been murdered because of her involvement with a Nazi spy ring operating in the early 1940s.

The source of this image is not known, and the Express and the Star archives no longer have a copy in their files, or any knowledge of its origin.

The other photograph, which has not been widely published,[21] is of the actual crime scene image. All the crime scene negatives have gone missing, leaving only photographic prints which are overexposed and out of focus. However, with the aid of computer software, the images have been enhanced and are now viewable.

Enhanced crime scene photograph exhibit Ref: HW/26.

[21] Earliest reference found in Bromsgrove Advertiser & Messenger 8th July, 1993, p.29.

The tree is described by Sergeant Skerratt[22] and Professor Webster[23] as "...being a hollow tree with the main trunk being 5½ feet high with the hollow or bole being lower down at about 3 ½ feet from the ground. The bole aperture was 24 inches at its widest points, the inside was funnel shaped, with the aperture reducing to 17 inches lower down."

Enhanced crime scene photograph exhibit Ref: HW/23.

Detective Superintendent Sidney Inight was the Senior Investigating Officer in charge of the police investigation into what was to be known formally as the Hagley Wood Murder. It would be the results of the forensic examination that would go on to influence the scope and direction of his investigation. This forensic examination was the task of Professor Webster, who attended the crime scene, assisted by Dr Lund back at the Birmingham Forensic Laboratory.

---

[22] Murder Casebook issue 71, (1991) p2536-41.
[23] Minutes of No.9 Regional Police Conference, 3rd May, 1943.

Professor Webster, on his retirement from the Birmingham laboratory in 1955, was described as "the greatest detective of them all.[24] His evidence sent more murders to the scaffold than any other pathologist in Britain,"[25] and he was described as "one of the most brilliant pathologists in Britain."[26]

Sidney William Inight Circa 1953.

The next three chapters will look at Professor Webster, Dr Lund, and the capability offered by the Birmingham Forensic Laboratory to assist with the investigation.

---

[24] Birmingham Mail 08.10.1955.
[25] Birmingham Gazette 08.10.1955.
[26] Glasgow Times 02/03/1956.

5
Professor Webster

James Mathewson (pronounced 'Matheson') Webster was born on the 27th January, 1898, at Alyth in Perthshire, Scotland. He died aged 75 on 17th November, 1973 at his home: 37 Beacon Hill, Rubery, Rednal, in the district of Bromsgrove, Birmingham.

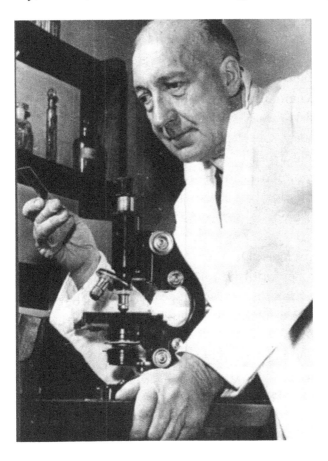

The only son of a Scottish Presbyterian Minister,[27] Webster was a classics scholar, educated at Dundee High School and St Andrews University, where he graduated with a MA in 1919 and a BSc with first-class honours in zoology and natural philosophy

---

[27] Dr Ben Davies, University of Birmingham Gazette, 1973, Vol. 27 pp.21-22.

in 1923. His passion was for English literature and language and as a young man, he played golf and water polo.

He was a large man;[28] he had a glass eye, having lost his own in a childhood accident, and he wore a monocle to enhance the vision in the remaining eye. He apparently enjoyed maintaining the myth that the Scots are tight with their money and was quoted as saying, "Och, a pair of glasses is no damn good to a man with a glass eye."

His first appointment was in 1924 at Chesterfield Royal Infirmary. This is where he first came to the attention of Percy Sillitoe, then Chief Constable of Chesterfield (who later became Director General of MI5 in 1946). In April 1924, a woman was attacked by a man with an axe at the Anchor Inn, Whittington Moor, near Chesterfield. The woman was admitted to Chesterfield Hospital where she came under the care of the newly-appointed resident surgeon, Dr Webster. The woman lay unconscious for two days and he stayed with her throughout, saving her life.

Once conscious, Dr Webster refused to allow the police to interview her until he felt she was well enough. This delay in gathering a statement was noticed by Percy Sillitoe, who went to the hospital to tackle this 'difficult' doctor himself. After being told Dr Webster was too busy to see him, he waited in the corridor and eventually confronted him. After a difficult introduction, they sat down to talk over a cup of tea in the hospital kitchen. Sillitoe was impressed by the young doctor's dedication and by his knowledge of the woman's injuries, and what had caused them. This was the start of what would become a lifelong friendship.

In 1926, during his three years at Chesterfield, Dr Webster obtained the Fellowship of the Royal College of Surgeons from Edinburgh. He then spent two years in general practice at

---

[28] Pugh J.M. (2005) p.11; Execution – One Man's Life And Death.

Redditch, following which he was appointed to the staff of the Smallwood Hospital. He also became a lecturer in anatomy at the Welsh National School of Medicine in Cardiff.

In 1929, Percy Sillitoe had left Chesterfield to become the Chief Constable in Sheffield. Forensic science was still in its infancy but Sillitoe was keen to develop a forensic science laboratory for his force. This was, in part, due to the short supply of expertise outside of London. The scientific investigation of crime at the time had been monopolised by the pathologists Sir Bernard Spilsbury (1877-1947), Sir Henry Willcox (1870-1941) and Professor Cedric Keith Simpson (1907-1985). They were all celebrities - adored by the public and press alike. They presided over the most horrific of crimes and their every word was accepted as gospel.

There were others who were also credited as being amongst the founders of forensic medicine, such as fellow Scotsman Dr Gerald Roche Lynch (1889-1957) and Dr J.H. Ryffel (1920-1955), both of whom worked for the Scotland Yard Laboratory. These experts were very expensive and were in constant demand. If unavailable, there was no one else able to assist the police.

Sheffield also needed a police surgeon—someone to undertake post-mortems of anyone whose death had not been natural, and who would help to realise Sillitoe's vision for a newly- created forensic facility.

On 1st April, 1929, Dr Webster was appointed police surgeon for Sheffield. He also became a lecturer in toxicology and forensic medicine at Sheffield University, as well as being credited with an article about Health Factors in the Modern Police Force.[29]

From small beginnings, a police laboratory was built. It was not the first in the country; Nottingham was also developing the

---

[29] Chief Constables' Association Annual Report 11th June, 1936, pp.47-57.

capability, whilst Derbyshire had begun a year earlier. However, the honour of being the first laboratory was enjoyed by the Hendon facility, which served Scotland Yard.

In 1936, local laboratories started to come under the control of the Home Office. The first regional laboratory was set up in Nottingham to serve the East Midlands area. This was led by Dr H.S. Holden - a former professor of botany at Nottingham University - along with around half a dozen staff, mostly from the university.

During the period the Nottingham laboratory was being established for the East Midlands; it was agreed that the West Midlands also required a laboratory. This was to be located on Newton Street in Birmingham, alongside the existing mortuary facilities.[30] The laboratory would not only serve Birmingham, but also the counties of Warwickshire, Worcestershire, Staffordshire and Shropshire. Notably, the Home Office was keen for the two laboratories to collaborate and develop specialist capabilities to aid each other and not to duplicate functions. Because Nottingham did not have a pathologist, it was agreed that the post of Director should be a pathologist; Dr Webster was identified as a suitable candidate for the appointment.

1937 was a significant year for Dr Webster. Firstly, on 7th April, plans for the laboratory were approved although the facility would not be occupied or fully staffed until February the following year. On 16th April, for a salary of £1,250 a year, Dr Webster became Director of this yet-to-be-built forensic laboratory. Until it was ready, he occupied an office within the Police Headquarters, which were also on Newton Street.

In June, Dr Webster joined the *exclusive pathology club* when he worked alongside the most best-known pathologist in the country at the time, Sir Bernard Spilsbury, on the famous murder

---

[30] Birmingham Post and Journal, 30/07/1936.

case of Frederick Nodder,[31] who was charged twice for the murder of a ten-year-old girl called Mona Tinsley. Dr Webster was asked to examine the remains of Mona in an outhouse, close to where her body was recovered from the river Idle, just downstream from the village of Bawtry.

Dr Webster was a prosecuting witness at the trial and by all accounts, he had a difficult time in the box. He gave evidence to the fact that the body had been in the water for five to six months, and that a mark around the child's neck was the result of a thin cord or string being tied about it before death. The defence argued that the mark could have been caused by the girl's clothing being caught in branches and wrapping around her neck. The jury came to the unanimous verdict of guilty, meaning the defendant was sentenced to death. On 30th December, 1937, Frederick Nodder was hanged at Lincoln Prison.

Miss Edith Smith circa 1955.

---

[31] Browne D.G. and Tullett T. (1981) Bernard Spilsbury), His Life and Cases, pp.312-318.

The first member of staff to join Dr Webster in Birmingham was Miss Edith Smith, his secretary. Her introduction to the job involved finding anatomical specimens on the desk where her typewriter should have been. "Don't worry about that Missie", Dr Webster would say. She didn't in fact worry, and remained working with him until his retirement.

Dr Webster finally took possession of the 'award winning' building[32] on 1st February, 1938. Dr Whithouse (chemist) joined his team on 8th February, followed by Mr Lund[33] (Biologist) on the 14th. Shortly afterwards, biology assistant Jack Merchant, Jack Hatton (lab boy), and Police Sergeant Burgess (who had come down from Sheffield as their liaison officer), also joined.

There was a formal inauguration of the facility on 3rd June, 1938[34] - of particular note is the fact that over these four months, only thirty cases had been completed. The laboratory's area of responsibility was then increased to include not only the East Midlands police forces as planned, but also South Wales.

There were several interesting police investigations which Dr Webster was involved with leading up to his attendance at Hagley Wood.

In March 1939,[35] the Irish Republican Army (IRA) started a bombing campaign, with devices going off at Coleshill's Hams Hall Power Station (the main source of Birmingham's electricity supply), and on an aqueduct serving Birmingham's canal system.

---

[32] 1938 RIBA bronze award, Messrs Peacock & Bewlay, best design in Birmingham.
[33] Joined straight from university and obtained his PhD in 1939.
[34] The watch committee reported on 7th July that the laboratory was operational.
[35] 1939-40 IRA Sabotage Campaign against the civil, economic, and military infrastructure of the UK.

The following months saw more bombings, including charges which exploded in the Paramount Cinema, as well as mail bombs which were detonated in a Birmingham mail lorry and various post boxes.

DR. J. H. WEBSTER

From South Wales Echo 30/09/1939

In September 1939, Dr Webster was also the pathologist on the inquiry into the unsolved murder of Joyce Cox, whose body was discovered by a railway embankment near Coryton station just days before her fifth birthday. This case was re-opened in 2017 by South Wales Police's Cold Case Unit.[36]

On 6th February, 1939, there was an explosion in a mailbag at the GPO on Hill Street, Birmingham. This occurred the day before two IRA men, James Richards and Peter Barnes (who had been found guilty of the previous bombings), were hanged at Birmingham's Winson Green prison. On 14th February, another five bombs exploded in Birmingham.

On 5th May, 1942, a six-year-old evacuee from London, Patricia Ann Cupitt, was murdered by James Wyeth in Riddlesworth,

---

[36] FOI MEPO 3/676 Metropolitan Police have refused to release reports until 2040, 100 years after the event.

near Thetford, Norfolk. Dr Webster gave evidence stating that the child was healthy and her death was due to violence. Wyeth was found guilty, although because he was classified insane, he was sent to Broadmoor.

In 1943, Dr Webster was appointed Professor of Forensic Medicine and Toxicology, and became known by employees and alike as 'Prof'. Shortly thereafter he was called in on the Hagley Wood murder case.

6
Dr John Lund

John Walter Guerrier Lund, CBE, DSc, FRS, FIBiol, FCIWEM, was born in Manchester on 27th November, 1912, and died, aged 102, on 21st March, 2015, at his home in Ambleside, Cumbria.[37] He was first taught at Sedbergh School, going on to study at Manchester University, where he gained his B.Sc. and M.Sc. degrees. In 1935, he moved to University College, London to work on benthic algae, gaining his PhD in 1939.

John Lund by Walter Bird ©Godfrey Argent Studio

On 14th February, 1938, Mr Lund joined the West Midlands Forensic Science Laboratory in Birmingham, working for several years as a forensic botanist.[38] In 1939, he was barred from war

---

[37] Obituary, Royal Society, 2015
[38] The Birmingham Home Office Forensic laboratory 1938-1988; Ref: MS4724, Birmingham Library Archive

service due to eyesight deficiencies, and obtained his PhD from the University of London. He was an expert scientific witness in courtroom trials and learnt to distinguish between convincing and unconvincing evidence although he felt he experienced adverse reactions from some judges, who had little respect for science. One judge even summed up by advising the jury to discount his scientific evidence.[39]

In 1944, he joined the staff of The Freshwater Biological Association, researching the ecology of planktonic algae in the English Lake District first at Wray Castle, and from 1950 at Ferry House. During this time, he worked with a fellow scientist, Hilda Canter, whom he later married.

Dr Lund became a Fellow of the Royal Society in 1963, and was awarded a CBE in 1965. He officially retired in 1978 as a Deputy Chief Scientific Officer, although he continued working for several days a week until 2005.

---

[39] *Biogr. Mems Fell. Royal Society* 2016 62, pp.345-358, published 18th November, 2015.

7
The Birmingham Forensic Laboratory

At the time of the Hagley Wood murder, the level of forensic science expertise within the Birmingham laboratory was minimal, in part, due to the newness of the profession, and because the authorities did not recognise forensic science as an entity. This was despite the fact that the facility had been designed as a national hub for pathology.[40]

The elite practise of forensic medicine (pathology and toxicology) had dominated the development of police laboratories until the late 1930s, when the Home Office regional laboratories were introduced. The older term, forensic medicine, was changed to forensic science to take into account all the new specialist disciplines available to investigators.

The Treasury had insisted that there should be no duplication of work within the regional laboratories; Birmingham was destined to be a centre for pathology, and the facility was initially designed to support that primary function.

The move away from forensic medicine to forensic sciences (also known briefly as Police Science)[41] was a relatively slow affair. Despite being a Home Office initiative, the government had made no formal provision for research or for training the new 'forensic scientists'. Before the laboratory system was established, analysts had taken on new tasks which stretched their expertise, meaning they were asked for their opinions on questions outside of their expertise.[42] This lack of experience did not go un-noticed; although Dr Webster escaped criticism. The same could not be

---

[40] J Ward (1993) 'Origins' pp.248-249: A.K. Mant (1973) 'A survey' p.22.

[41] From the French *Police Scientifique*.
[42] JB Firth (1960) 'A scientist' p.19.

said for Dr Roche Lynch from the Scotland Yard laboratory. It is reported that he was persuaded, disastrously, to undertake glass, hair, fibres, dust and blood-grouping work, of which he had no experience whatsoever'.[43]

As well as a lack of experience, the move to Home Office-funded laboratories also raised concerns that bias would be a problem, as the service was no longer independent[44] from the central prosecution. Instead, it could be seen as being 'hand in glove' with the prosecution, meaning laboratories[45] might be "compelled to produce evidence in favour of the police case."

Another issue which apparently caused aggravation amongst Dr Webster's fellow Directors was a benefit within his condition of employment. Although the general rule was that pathologists would only be paid where work resulted in a guilty plea, whilst at Sheffield Webster received neither court nor post-mortem fees.[46] He addressed this issue on his appointment to Birmingham; the result being an entitlement to retain fees in respect of post-mortem examinations he undertook, on top of his basic salary.

Not all forensic activity moved to the regional laboratories. Police forces had been following New Scotland Yard's lead, building fingerprint and photographic capabilities since the early 1900s. In 1933, Sergeant Sidney Inight and DC Thomas Williams were responsible for setting up the Worcestershire Constabulary Fingerprint and Photographic Bureau.[47]

On 1st February, 1938, Dr Webster took up his new position at the Birmingham Laboratory. The office hours were weekdays

[43] J Ward (1993) 'Origins' p.250.
[44] K Layborn D Taylor (2011) 'Policing' p.98.
[45] Ambage, 'Origins', p.123
[46] NV Ambage, 'Origins', pp.52-5.

[47] B Pooler (2002) 'A History' p.122.

from 9 a.m. to 5.30 p.m., and 9 a.m. to 1 p.m. on Saturdays. It would be several years before the case load would break the 400 barrier, and so the staff used their spare time to build a reference library of control slides of hair, fibres, paper, buttons and matches. They also spent time visiting police forces to promote the service; and to deliver a lecture entitled 'Dust, dirt, debris, hair, fibres and cellulosic material'

In 1939, at the start of World war Two, the laboratory equipment was fairly limited, consisting of standard glassware, four microscopes, a microtome slicer, an absorptiometer for measuring pressure, a camera attachment used for microphotography, a Spectrograph and a Marsh Apparatus for arsenic analysis.

On 10th April, 1941, the laboratory was damaged during an air raid, with all of the windows being blown out. The premises were patched up and the laboratory continued its work throughout the war. In 1945, the building was seen as in need of urgent repair, but it would be 1949 before any repair work would be carried out.

As of 1943, the laboratory was staffed[48] by Professor Webster, Miss Smith (Personal Assistant), Dr Whithouse[49] (Chemist), Dr Lund[50] (Biologist), Jack Merchant (Experimental Assistant Grade 3), Jack Hatton (Lab Boy), Chief Inspector Burgess (Police Liaison Officer) and Mrs Aims (Cleaner).

It is easy to say that things would be done differently today - that's a fact. The level of expectation placed on Webster and his small team was considerable. They did their best with the wartime resources available, whilst some of the experts who would now be brought in to assist with a similar investigation,

---

[48] Home Office Staff List August 1944.
[49] Left 1945 – joined Mitchells & Butler Brewery.
[50] Left 1944 – joined the Freshwater Biological Association.

were yet to be classed as forensic experts in the 1940s. This included professionals who conduct crime scene recovery, Crime Scene Investigators and specialist search teams.

8
At the Crime Scene

The official tools which help to describe a crime scene are images, referencing the investigators' initial observations, lists of what was and was not recovered from the crime scene; and the scientific interpretations.

On 19th and 20th April, the scene was photographed and one or more crime scene photographic booklets[51] were produced by DI Williams. On 21st April, Dr Lund provided a statement on his examination of the clothing. This was followed by a laboratory statement on 23rd April from Professor Webster. The fourth and, in my opinion, the most significant document comprises the Minutes of the No.9 Regional Conference held in Birmingham on 3rd May, 1943. The reason is that, at this meeting, Professor Webster expanded and clarified some of the observations made in his earlier statement. However, by then, the earlier findings had already influenced the direction of the investigation and been widely reported, both in police circles and in the media. The minutes provide the most useful source for the Bella narrative to date. Finally, there are two additional laboratory-generated artefacts. These include photographic images taken by Professor Webster[52] of the skeletal remains, the ring and shoes, and a picture board of the clothing credited to Dr Lund. The statements from 21st and 23rd April, and the minutes from 3rd May, are transcribed in full at the end of this publication for reference. The other images are presented alongside the storyline.

Missing from this collection is the coroner's inquest report from 28th April, which could have provided some additional

---

[51] Exhibit Ref: HW1-HW45, photographs of the Wych Elm: Worchester Constabulary Photographs; Wych Elm tree at Hagley Wood, Det Insp TN Williams, 19th & 20th April, 1943.
[52] File16/158 Date 3/5.43 Copy of photographs taken by Professor Webster in Hagley Wood murder.

background. Records archived with the Worcestershire Coroner are only maintained for fifteen years. A search of the official archive yielded nothing, and newspaper articles make reference only to the verdict.

The following chapters draw from these official documents, as well as other referenced published accounts. I will present the sequence of events, unpick the observations, and deliberate on other possibilities and further research.

It had been standard police practice since the 1930s that in a murder case, nothing should be disturbed until a Police Surgeon had inspected the scene and photographs taken.[53] DI Williams attended the crime scene on 19th and 20th April, and produced a booklet containing forty-five photographs.

The black and white photographs would have been taken to the Photographic Department at Hindlip Hall to be developed and printed.[54] There are several stages during this process where things could (and did) go wrong. Ultimately, it is only when the development and printing process is finished that one knows if the photography has been successful. If a problem arises (as in this case), one cannot return to the scene of the crime as it wouldn't be the same as when the pictures were first taken, everything significant having been recovered.

Despite many images being of poor quality, DI Williams must have had something of value in order to produce a booklet.

Of the forty-five photographs, all that remains in the files held at the Worcestershire Archive is an album cover and nineteen loose photographs. Of these, sixteen are referenced and three are not. Furthermore, of the nineteen photographs, only nine, after digital enhancement, are of value for republication.

---

[53] Percy Sillitoe (1955) Cloak Without Dagger, p.74.
[54] The negatives would have been filed at Harpley Hall.

REF	View	Observation
Photographic Booklet (Hagley Wood) Ref: HW1-HW45 Photographs of the Wych Elm DI Williams 19th-20th April, 1943		
HW/1-HW/15	Missing	The sequence would indicate images possibly taken on the 19th.
HW/16-HW/21	Inside the hollow	HW/16, HW/19 & HW/20 enhanced and of value.
HW/22-HW/27	View of tree (from same direction)	HW/23 & HW/26 enhanced and of value.
HW/28-HW/31	View of cutaway tree	HW/31 enhanced and of value.
HW/32-HW/45	Missing; less three unmarked or referenced photographs	(1) Skull and jaw being held front view. (2) Skull and jaw side profile. (3) Bone on the ground.

HW/26 shows the approach route to the tree

The tree is alive and in early leaf; bluebells are visible and in flower, and the surrounding area is covered in young undergrowth, corresponding with the season as well as the description reported.

The bole aperture is visible in this enhanced and cropped image; the opening was 24 inches at its widest points.

Faced with this view, Professor Webster considered whether the cause of death was accident, suicide, or murder. He concluded murder over the other two propositions, stating "the entrance to this tree was extremely narrow and would have caused not merely inconvenience, but actual injury if even a small woman of this nature should have forced herself into the tree. Further, I do not think that this was a likely position for committing suicide.

Accident can, I think, be entirely ruled out. The tree, however, afforded an excellent concealment for murder."

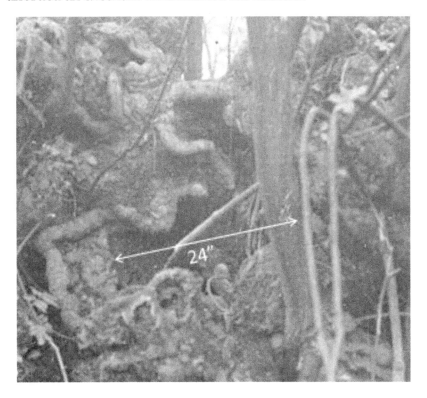

Webster then goes on to say that "from the position of the skeleton in the bole of the tree, I am of the opinion that this woman was pushed in feet first. Moreover, she could only have been pushed in conveniently either before rigor mortis set in or after rigor mortis had passed off. If the body had been kept until rigor mortis had passed off, putrefaction would have commenced, and it is extremely unlikely that the murderer would have kept the body until it had got into this condition. Hence I am of the opinion that this body was pushed into the tree before rigor mortis had set in. This being so, it is likely that the murder was committed in near vicinity to the tree, or, if committed at a distance, the murderer must have had a conveyance to enable him to get the body to the tree before rigor mortis set in."

The Professor also states that "the wood is well known to many people and the tree in which the body was hidden was the best and indeed the only place where a body could be hidden in the wood. The use of such a place of concealment would appear to indicate local knowledge."

There is another possibility that Professor Webster does not include within his findings, and which I believe is worthy of consideration. Rather than being placed inside the tree shortly after her death, Bella could have been killed and hidden somewhere else first. Following this, at a later date, her decomposed remains could have been moved and hidden in the tree. This is sometimes known in the jargon of today as a 'secondary dump-site'.

If this was true, it would mean that, even if the calculations regarding the length of time that the remains had been concealed in the tree are correct, it would be necessary to revise the time and location of the murder, as well as the scope of the police investigation.

HW/19 & HW/20, enhanced images.

The next sequence of images includes enhanced areas from photographs HW/19 and HW/20, showing views of interest.

The skull is lying on a thick blanket of debris with some bones visible underneath. The size and volume of the twigs could be an indication that the offender(s) concealed the remains from view with leaf debris. As well as this, there is no visible tree or vegetation growing within the hollow.

Lying on top of the debris is the right shoe (with partial laces), clean of any debris and with no bones visible inside. Bob Farmer indicates that he saw a pair of shoes and a green bottle[55] inside the hollow. Professor Webster reports that, "...it would appear probable that the pair of shoes, one recovered from the bole of the tree, and the other at some distance,[56] are connected with this body."

It is not clear why or how he concluded that they belonged to Bella. If Bella had been wearing them at the time she was placed into the tree, they would realistically have been under the leaf debris and skeleton, and if worn, should have contained ankle and foot bones. Even if they had been placed inside loose, at the same time as Bella, their locations and condition are unusual.

---

[55] There is no bottle visable on the photographs or referenced in any official report.
[56] Express and Star 24/04/1943 reports that the other shoe was 100 feet away.

HW/28

To access the remains, a side section of the trunk was removed by Constable Pound, in the area used as the approach route. The only remaining photographs (HW/28-31) of the 'cut-away' were taken after the contents were recovered - again nothing visible and no reference to vegetation or growth.

The analysis of the bones and clothing was undertaken back at the Birmingham laboratory, although Professor Webster recorded some of his observations at the scene.

It was approximately 6.30 p.m. when he was able to recover the remains, stating that "...the skull was in two parts, consisting of the head, which lay exposed on the floor of the tree bole, and the lower jaw, which was in line with the disarticulated vertebrae (spine) under the overhanging entrance to the hollow bole." He also observes that "tightly pressed over the lower jaw in the cavity of the mouth I found part of the khaki or mustard coloured dress which the deceased was wearing at the time of death. So far as this thrust over the teeth margin and so firmly adherent to the teeth was this part of the apparel that I do not consider it likely – I cannot say impossible – that this came into the mouth accidentally after death. It appears much more probable that this had been forced into the mouth prior to death, and, if so, this would have been capable of causing death from asphyxia."

Furthermore, he goes on to say, "I recovered from the debris below the lower jaw a small piece of thin fragile bone which in my opinion constitutes one of the cornua of a human hyoid bone. The rest of the hyoid was missing, and this might well be accounted for by the ravages of animals. Both pelvic bones have suffered considerably from the ravages of animals, and small parts of them are missing."

The formation and distribution of the skeleton was also described: "...from the position of the bones, the woman was not lying flat down but in a semi-reclining position. When the head rotted off and dropped down then the rest of the trunk dropped down."

Much of the material in the hollow was in an advanced state of decomposition. Despite not being visible in any of the photographs, there is reference to considerable and extensive growth of the tree roots, intertwining through the remainder of the clothing.

Twelve yards from the tree, the official record indicates that they recovered a human tibia or shin bone. Certain references[57] state that these bones were "...hidden amongst the roots of saplings, along with some scraps of clothing nearby." Could this be the source of the references to tree root growth?

There is no reference in the official documentation to the recovery of a severed right hand[58] and/or "...some smaller bones

---

[57] McCormick p.60.
[58] Coley p.5, Sparke p.5.

of the skeleton, including those of the fingers of one hand."[59] However, such references later appear in many publications. This has become known as 'The Hand of Glory', with many linking it to witchcraft.

The next day, more bones were recovered and sent to the laboratory: a left pelvic bone, a right femur, and a right fibula. In addition a rolled gold enamel ring was recovered.

There are three additional photographs which remain from the HW/32-45 group. One is of a bone on the ground and two are of the skull and jaw - of note is the fact that the material tightly pressed against the jaw is not visible despite still being in place when Dr Lund undertook his examination later back in the laboratory.

Later, after the skeleton was examined, it was found to be incomplete. Missing, and possibly still in Hagley Wood (or at another crime scene) are: the right tibia or shin bone, part of the hyoid bone, a patella, some of the small bones of the hands and

[59] McCormick p.88.

feet, and two teeth (the upper left lateral incisor, and the second right molar).

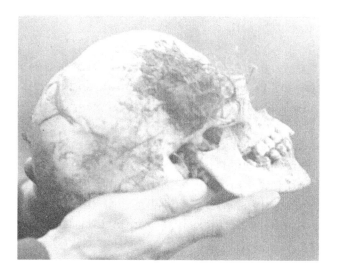

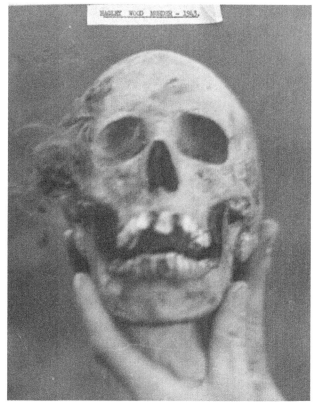

In addition to the material already found, the search party recovered some clothing on the southern boundary of the wood. However, it was reported in 1949 that this clothing had been discarded over the hedge, into Hagley Wood, by two Gypsy families - the Smiths and the Butlers - as they vacated the Nimmings field (plot 5) site in December 1942. It was also reported that "...the clothing had been taken to Stourbridge Police Station but by 1949 had rotted and is not to be found in Stourbridge."[60]

The recovered bones and clothing were taken to the Birmingham laboratory for examination and analysis, with Dr Lund taking possession of the exhibits on the evening of 20th April.[61]

---

[60] Report Superintendent TN Williams, 05/10/1949.

[61] Steve Punt (2015) Punt PI, broadcast 6th August, BBC Radio 4 Who Put Bella in The Wych Elm?

9
Bodies in Small Spaces

Putting bodies in small places has been fashionable since the early 1900s, when the public became fascinated and horrified by the concealment method used by murderers - known as 'trunk murders'. The first occurred in 1905 when Arthur Devereux murdered his wife and twin children, whom he packed in (what he thought was) an air-tight container; he then sent them to a furniture storage warehouse. Following this, there was the 1927 Charing Cross trunk case, in which the remains of Mrs Bonati were found. In 1934, the same scenario was re-enacted, although this time in Brighton, with other body parts turning up at King's Cross and Charing Cross railway stations in London.

Several accounts of the Bella story suggest putting a body in a tree was an unusual occurrence - for Professor Webster and the team, whilst a tree concealment was extraordinary, bodies in small and unusual spaces were not.

The 'trunk murders' were at the extreme end of this concealment type, although bodies hidden in cupboards and wardrobes were and remain a common feature of murder investigations.

The entrance to the tree was extremely narrow; it was a 'letter box' opening, twenty-four inches by twelve inches, with part of the tree acting as an overhang. The hollow opened out into a cone shape inside, with the base decreasing to seventeen inches in diameter. It was three and a half feet in height, meaning that Bella would have filled almost all available space, leaving approximately one foot of space at the top.

Getting into the hollow would have been difficult. This fact is acknowledged by Professor Webster in reference to a live person getting into the tree: "it would have caused not merely inconvenience, but actual injury if even a small woman of this nature should have forced herself into the tree." Because of this, as well as the position of the skeleton, he was of the opinion that Bella must have been pushed into the tree feet first when dead; however, this would have happened before rigor mortis set in, or later, after rigor mortis passed.

Decomposition and skeletonisation is affected by a considerable number of factors, including temperature, humidity, and the presence of insects and animals. Time assumptions are also complicated further by the fact that the hollow would have had its own micro-climate - sheltered from the elements due to its small opening and its seasonal leaf covering. For this reason, it could have taken many years for Bella to become a skeleton.

The first stage in the process is known as rigor mortis — the term used to describe stiffening of the limbs. In an average environment, rigor mortis starts within one to four hours; first in the jaw and smaller limbs, followed by the arms, then finally the legs after between four and six hours. Rigor mortis is complete after around twelve hours. If getting the body inside the tree was difficult enough whilst still flexible, it would have been impossible once rigor had set in. This condition remains until decomposition begins approximately twenty-four to fifty hours later, and with it the stiffness subsides.

After rigor mortis diminished, another opportunity to set the body inside the tree would have arisen. This said, however, the completion of rigor mortis would have been followed by the commencement of putrefaction. It was thought extremely unlikely that the murderer would have kept the body until it had got into that condition. As such, the investigators stuck with the 'before rigor' scenario, with the Professor deducing "it was likely that the murder was committed in the near vicinity to the tree, or, if committed at a distance, the murderer must have had a conveyance to enable him to get the body to the tree before rigor mortis set in."

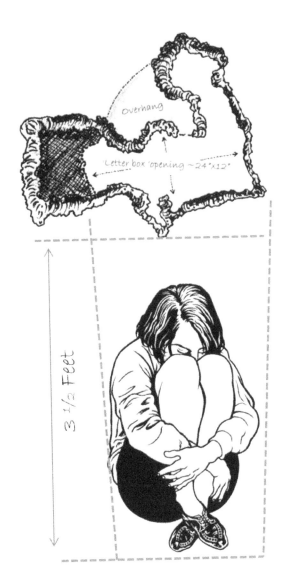

The putrefaction phase is also associated with a foul cocktail of smells, as organs liquify and the gasses (carbon monoxide, hydrogen sulphide and methane) are released. The fact that there would have been a foul smell was not lost on the investigation team, and there are multiple references where the absence of any smell is questioned in recorded statements. I only found one positive reference[62] to a nasty smell and I refer to that later on.

---

[62] Statement Mrs PM Tate, taken by Sergeant Skerrett, 28/09/1949.

In addition to the smell, a decomposing body also attracts insects at different intervals. This starts with flies: in an average environment, they can transform from eggs, to maggots, to winged insects in twenty-one to twenty-four days. During this period, other insect predators which feed on the maggots arrive, as do colonising insects, beetles, ants and wasps. In addition, mammals such as rodents, cats, dogs, foxes and even rabbits will scavenge on a corpse.

This provides a period of time where it would not be unreasonable to suggest that the tree would have seen considerable fly activity and been very smelly. Given its extremely close proximity to the track, these smells should have come to the notice of those passing by or in the wood foraging.

By the time Bella was found, the professor indicates that the "bones were completely stripped of flesh, and they may have remained in a dried condition for years." He also references the considerable growth of the roots of the tree through the remainder of the clothing and, taking that into consideration, concludes that Bella must have been there for a minimum period of eighteen months. Significantly, he also states that she "may have been there for a very considerably longer period."

The skeletisation phase[63] is also influenced by environmental conditions, which explains the various timings offered by the professor. His conclusion that the bones were completely stripped is, in my opinion, significant. Whilst soft tissue will have vanished within one or two years, layers of clothing (and shoes) can help preserve skin and some underlying tissue. Tendons, ligaments and cartilage survive longest, alongside inert elements such as hair and nails. This all points to the remains being older than previously reported.

---

[63] Bernard Knight, Forensic Medicine p.43.

10
The Shoes

The skeleton and clothing arrived at the laboratory on the evening of 20th April. Whilst the clothing was given to Dr Lund for examination, Professor Webster dealt with the skeleton and shoes.

A few days later, the shoes were handed over to Inspector Williams, who was tasked with investigating the source of manufacture and their distribution. Of particular note is a statement within Professor Webster's autopsy report, dated 23rd April, in which he concludes that "...these shoes are black shoes, size 5 ½, and from the information which I obtained, are probably made by Waterfoot Company." This indicates that, prior to the 23rd, he had already obtained some information about the shoes. If that information had been the possible year of manufacture, such knowledge could have influenced the laboratory findings—specifically his and Dr Lund's opinions on the time (and season) of the murder—as well as the style and period of the clothing worn.

The crime scene shoes were photographed. Three photographs remain within the archive files at Worchester, together with another image of a similar shoe presumably intended for the purpose of comparison.

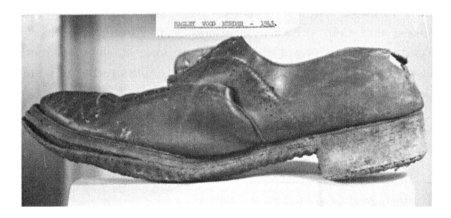

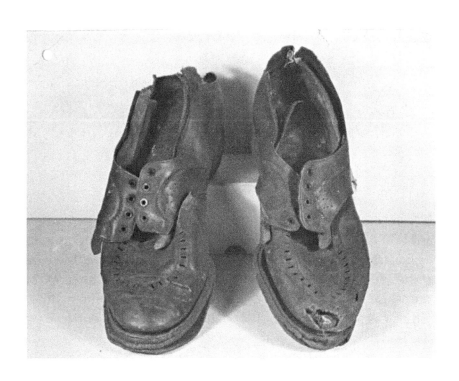

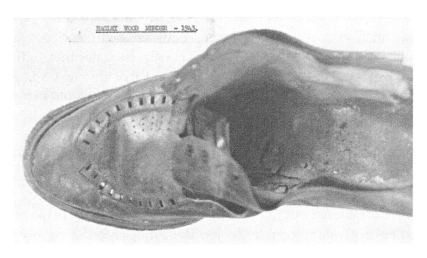

At 9.30 a.m. on 23rd April, DI Williams attended the laboratory and took possession of the shoes from Professor Webster. He was given a letter of introduction from Mr Alan Gordon Barnes, the secretary of the Northampton Boot and Shoe Manufactures Association.

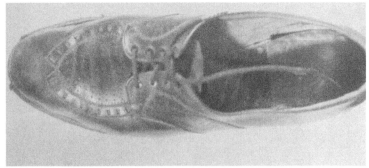

Additional photograph of similar shoe – possibly a prop.

By 11.30 a.m., Williams arrived in Northampton, meeting with Mr Barnes, who made several observations. He felt that the type of the shoe meant that it was manufactured in an area in Lancashire—known in the trade as the 'valley'—in a Rossendale district called Waterfront (the 'valley' would turn out to be a false lead).

There were also other observations. The shoes were not black but blue; it was felt that they had "seen six months hard ware", and the retail cost was somewhwere between eight and sixteen shillings (which was revised later). Finally, he states that "...the shoe size was 5 ½ English standard" and that this was a large shoe for a woman of five feet; he also states that he would expect a woman of that size to wear size 4 to 4 ½. As I will be discussing in a later chapter, Bella was actually shorter than five feet and accordingly her expected shoe size range was actually between 3 ½ and 4.

There is no reference to the shoe being 'packed out' to help with fitting but other than Inspector Williams' report, I have not uncovered any formal documentation reflecting the observation that the shoes were too big for Bella.

Mr Barnes was also asked to comment on the possible length of time the shoes had been exposed to the weather. Unable to offer an opinion, he directed Inspector Williams to the British Boot,

Shoe and Allied Trades Research Association at Kettering.[64] I was unable to find any official documentation referencing this line of inquiry, and the Association does not hold any archive material.

Finally, on 1st May, Inspector Williams attended Clarence Bray Limited at Sileby, Nr Loughborough, Leicester[65]. The shoe was recognised; the company's record book identified it as D.956 — "a blue semi-chrome side Gibson Shoe, with three rows of pin punching on quarter and vamp. It was made on a 97 last with leather through crepe sole and fair stitched fore part, and crepe heel." They confirmed that this type of shoe was manufactured between April and June, 1940. Also identified were the companies which the size 5 ½s were supplied to. C.A. Allan Ltd. of Bilston, Staffordshire received six pairs; seventy-two pairs were supplied to a mail order firm called Messrs Ambrose Wilson Ltd of London, and fifty-four pairs went to Messrs. Darnell & Son in Shoreditch, London, who were suppliers themselves.[66]

It was indicated that the retail price in 1940 for these shoes would have been thirteen shillings and eleven pence - around forty-eight pounds and seventy pence[67] in today's money.

Armed with this information, the investigators concentrated their inquiry on the local area. On 4th May,[68] Inspector Williams visited shops owned by Messrs C.A. Allen Limited in Bilston, Wednesbury and West Bromwich.

At the Wednesbury shop, he met with the owner Mr Allen, who indicated that the blue coloured shoe was known in the trade as

---

[64] Then at 30-36 Thorngate Street, Kettering. Now known as SATRA Technology.
[65] DI Williams, report dated 2nd May, inquiry regarding lady's shoes found in wood.
[66] Bray Ltd supplied four dealers, only three ordered size 5 ½.
[67] The National Archives Currency Convertor 2005.
[68] DI Willams report dated 5th May, 1943, inquiry Re Lady's Shoes.

'ice'. He explained it was a popular type which sold quickly, meaning that it would have been sold around June 1940.

Significantly, reference is yet again made to the fact that the shoes "were rather large for a woman of five feet." Therefore, if the shoes had been sold in June and endured six months' wear (as previously indicated) the earliest 'age in the tree' for the shoes would be December 1940—two years and three months before the discovery.

Professor Webster and the police were of the opinion that the shoes belonged to the victim. This is despite the fact that, within the shoes, there was no recovery or reporting of bones, flesh, leaf debris, material from socks, stockings, or padding to help with fitting. This opens up another possibility: that the shoes are not directly related to Bella at all; instead, they are in fact replacements (along with other items) designed to confuse the investigators.

What interested me most was trying to find out if the age of the shoes was known to the laboratory when they started to piece together what Bella was wearing. Did that knowledge bias their opinion to a specific style and period? Did they ignore the obvious and justify their observations by making Bella out to be "neglectful as to her appearance and habits", her social status and the 'make do and mend' culture because her shoes and clothing did not fit?

11
The Clothing and Hair

Dr Lund provided an independent report dated 21st April for the clothing and hair; his findings were incorporated into Professor Webster's autopsy report, dated 23rd April. Later, the Professor states[69] that, "Coming to the clothing, to a great extent I am indebted to Special Constable Goldfar in this matter." This provides an indication that expert advice on the clothing had been sought. Mr John Stewart Golfar[70] was a Special Constable, as well as the owner of a gown, dresses and children's clothing manufacturing business, with premises at 51 Mansfield Road, Aston in Birmingham.

Dr Lund notes that the material was in an advanced state of decomposition: it was not possible to produce more than part of a garment. Mr Golfar and Dr Lund identified five items of clothing: a pair of knickers, an underskirt, a corset, a skirt, and a cardigan with a knitted belt.

At the case conference on 3rd May, drawings of the clothing and cloth examples were presented. There was a request[71] for a colour photograph of a woman dressed as the victim to be circulated. Professor Webster commented on the difficulty of securing coloured prints, and it appears that this never happened.

Underskirt or Slip: Described as "artificial silk taffeta material, such as is used to line coats and costumes. This material is sometimes made up into very cheap underskirts or taken from coats and made up in the home. Although this material seems somewhat long for a woman of 5 feet, and although I have been unable to find any trace of shoulder straps, I am of the opinion that this is part of an underskirt and that in all probability the

---

[69] Minutes of No.9 Regional Conference, 3rd May, 1943, p.7
[70] Evening Dispatch 12th May, 1942: & 26th May, 1942.
[71] Sergeant Gwilliam (Wolverhampton).

garment was home-made. If it was the lining of a coat, then every trace of that coat has disappeared, which, in view of the state of preservation of the other garments, is most likely. In early statements the original colour of this garment is described as probably peach or, less likely, pink."

Later the professor changes his mind and states that the garment was dark peach or fawn; however, he favours a fawn colour. He adds some more detail: "It was, at least, a home-made slip and most of it was gone. We have only a large piece from the back. It is cheap material and the interesting thing about it is that if it had been worn by the woman without a tuck, it would have shown under the skirt and had been hemmed at the top and bottom by hand."
Inspector Williams suggested that it might be part of a nightdress worn by the woman under her clothing at the time of an air raid.

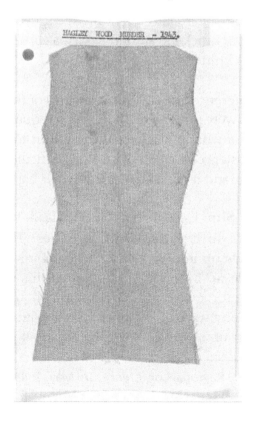

Knickers: Recovered were portions of a pair of navy blue interlock cotton knickers, described as a "cheap type of knicker."

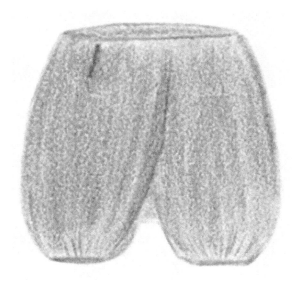

Corset: All that was recovered were portions of the metal stays, metal front and suspenders of a corset. Apart from a very small fragment of material attached to the metal front, the fabric had rotted away, and hence it is very difficult to deduce much as to its quality. The metal portions were, however, identical to those used in the 'wrap-round' type of corset which sold for between eight and ten shillings. It was initially thought more likely to have been that kind of corset rather than the heavy, old-fashioned type. This was later clarified, with the professor stating that, "The corset or corselet is definitely not old-fashion. It is a sort of corselet which fastens in front and has one or two stays to support it. It is a corselet rather than a corset. Her corsets or corselets would however, have the effect of pulling the slip under the hem of the skirt." He was also of the opinion that the presence of corsets suggests that Bella was not a young girl.

Skirt: The material which was thought to have been used to asphyxiate the victim was identified as being the lower portion of a good-class, all-wool garment, believed to almost certainly be a skirt with a side metal zip fastening.[72] The original colour was thought to probably be mustard or pale khaki, perhaps with a tinge of beige.

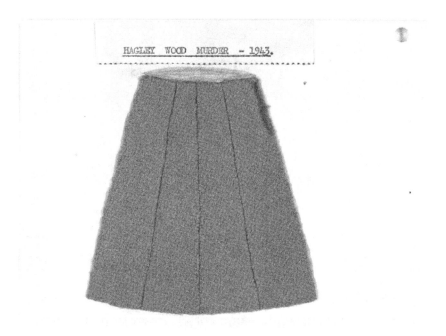

HAGLEY WOOD MURDER – 1943.

Cardigan: The cardigan was described as a knitted woollen cardigan with alternating pale khaki or mustard coloured (presumably to match the skirt) and dark blue stripes. Also recovered were five cloth-covered buttons and a knitted wool belt of a somewhat brighter blue than that of the cardigan itself.

The metal portion of a belt buckle was also present; there was no cloth attached to it and they thought it extremely unlikely that it was covered. Significantly, Dr Lund reports that there was no sign of any sleeves on the garment. However, he felt that this type of cardigan commonly had long sleeves. Why they decided on a long sleeve top rather than a sleeveless waistcoat or 'tank top' style is not clear.

---

[72] During WW2 they stopped using metal zips to help the war effort and elastic was rationed.

He goes on to report that the cardigan was of quite a good material and was of the ribbed variety. It consisted of five ribs in one-inch navy, with three ribs making up half an inch in mustard or khaki colour.

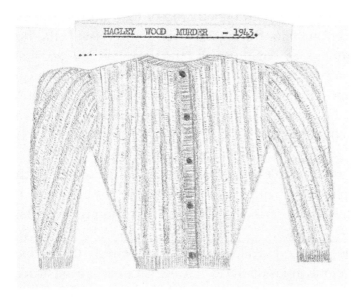

HAGLEY WOOD MURDER — 1943.

Dr Lund produced two images of what he felt the cardigans may have looked like, but did not indicate which one he believed to be correct.

Professor Webster also states, "There was no sign of any stockings, and therefore, as the case of the coat, I am of the opinion that there were none. There was no trace of stockings whatsoever. So far as weathering is concerned, while a great deal of the stockings might have gone, you would have had surviving some of the cotton. I am satisfied that she was not wearing stockings at the time." Based on this fact, and the statements related to the other clothing assumptions, he goes on to presume that as this was all the clothing Bella was wearing. It seems clear that she was lightly dressed for outdoors, which suggests summer wear. He also observes that the general quality of the garments was poor.

The Hair: As well as the clothing, Dr Lund was tasked with looking at the hair. He observed that a large quantity of head hair had been recovered, and that it was very brittle and in a rotted state. It was impossible to tell what kind of hair style Bella had, but there was no sign of permanent waving; it had not been dyed or bleached, and a few grey hairs were present. It was thought that she had a good crop of light 'mousy' brown hair. However, in 1956, during a television interview,[73] the Professor was quoted as saying that "the girl had ginger hair". No explanation was given for this change of opinion. If true, during decomposition, dark hair often looks ginger, because the brown pigment is less stable than the red pigment, and so Bella may still have had dark hair.

It was not possible to be accurate about the length of the hair, although a few hairs measured seven inches in length. For this reason, it was described as "neither very short nor very long."

At this point, I will introduce an image that appears in publications and is often referenced[74] in police reconstructions of Bella. It first appeared in Donald McCormick's book, Murder by

---

[73] 22nd May, 1956

[74] Coley p.7, Sparke p.7, McCormick p.88 (fingers) p.98 (reconstruction).

Witchcraft – a study of the lower Quinton and Hagley Wood murders published in 1968. It also appeared in the Birmingham Daily Post newspaper,[75] within an article written by McCormick, who was advertising his book. I have been unable to find any earlier reproductions of this image prior to 1968.

Donald McCormick's 1968 reconstruction of Bella.

Of particular note is the reference to "noticeably irregular front teeth and lower jaw", which is discussed in the following

---

[75] Birmingham Daily Post 20/08/68.

chapter, as well as the different styles of interpretation and pattern design and colours of the clothing.

In addition to introducing an image of Bella, McCormick also referenced the finger bones of one hand being buried some distance from the tree - and introduced witchcraft into the story.

12

The Bones

Professor Webster reconstructed the skeleton; he made observations, took photographs and reported his findings on 23rd April. He also produced a photographic booklet: File Number 15/158 dated 3rd May, 1943. The front cover indicates that he provided eleven photographs (referenced HW/46 – HW/56) and two negatives. The booklet provided three images at various exposures: of the skeleton, lower jaw and a frontal dental view. As with the scene photographs, they are held loose at the Worcestershire Archive.

Photographic Booklet File Ref: 15/158 HW/46-HW/56 +Two Negatives Professor Webster 3rd May, 1943		
REF	View	Observation
HW/46-HW/49	Skeleton	Four photographs and one negative.
HW/50-HW/55	Lower Jaw	Six photographs and one negative.
HW/56	Frontal Dental	One photograph.

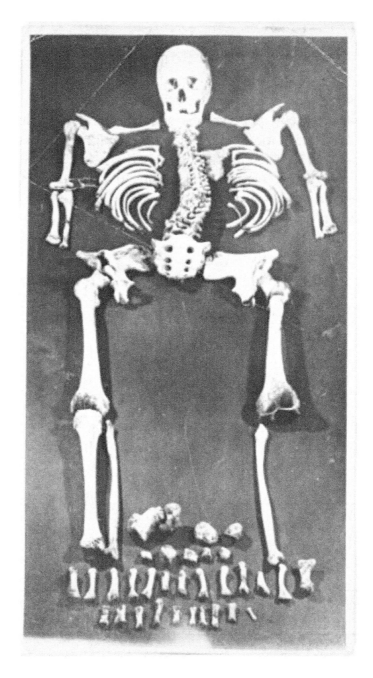

HW/46-49

HW/50-55

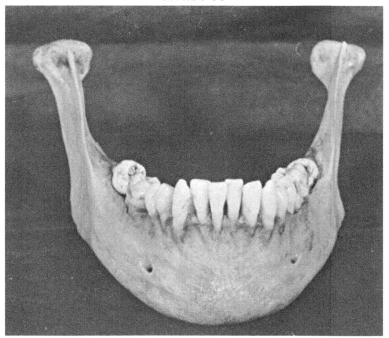

HW/56

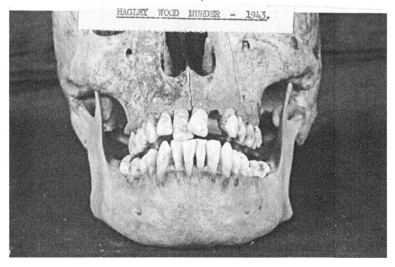

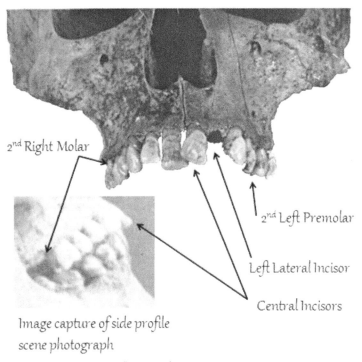

2nd Right Molar

2nd Left Premolar

Left Lateral Incisor

Central Incisors

Image capture of side profile
scene photograph

Extracts from reports[76]:

Teeth - Upper Jaw: In the upper jaw, the left lateral incisor and
the second right molar were missing. He notes that they had
dropped out post-mortem and were present in the head at the
time of death. Consequently, there is a realistic expectation that
they should have been recovered from inside the tree or the
surrounding area (if they fell out whilst being handled). Like the
missing bones, they could, however, be at another crime scene, or
may have even been removed by the offender(s) (if they had
been gold capped or had fillings) in an attempt to avoid
identification.

He goes on to report that the teeth were in good, clean condition,
except for the second left premolar, which showed signs of
decay.

---

[76] Statements: Professor Webster, 23rd April, 1943 and Case conference, 3rd
May. Both reproduced at the end of the book.

In addition, noticeable in the upper jaw, the central incisors were crooked and protruding. This would have been an obvious facial feature; however, this was not reported to the investigation team, nor did it feature in the initial dental inquiry.

Teeth - Lower Jaw: When Professor Webster discusses the lower jaw, he indicates that it was in fairly good condition; however, the first left molar was extremely decayed, whilst the first right molar had been extracted a considerable time before death. In the lower jaw, he observes that there was slight overlapping of the incisors. The best way he can think of describing these incisor teeth, "...is that there would have been a noticeable irregularity of the incisors." However, the question must be asked: why only reference the incisors in the lower jaw in his autopsy report on 23rd April, whilst those in the upper jaw are not explained?

The Dental Inquiry: The first formal request that investigators made for dental inquires appeared in the national publication 'Police Report' issue No.92 item 42, dated 11th May, 1943, where the lower jaw photograph (HW/50-55) is reproduced.

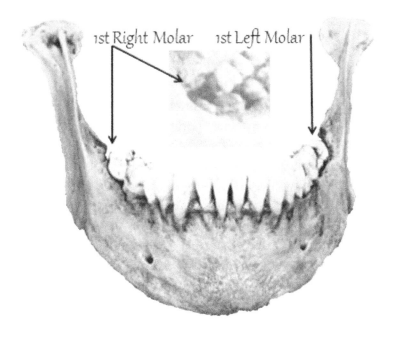

1st Right Molar   1st Left Molar

There had been previous Bella entries in the Police Report. The first (text only) report, on 29th April in issue No.84, item 17 provided a description of the victim, stating that there was "...no undue prominence of the teeth but noticeable irregularity of the front teeth in the lower jaw."

Issue No.85, item 1 (text only) on 30th April, reported the outcome of the inquest on 28th April, and repeated the previous description.

However, on 4th May, issue No.87, item 26, was the first publication to reproduce an image, not of the teeth, but of the recovered ring.

26—Worcestershire. Worcester (Co.).—85 Issue, 1 Report—Photo of:

Faceted wedding ring found near skeleton.
Police Report Issue No.87 item 26.

On 3rd May, a case conference was held in Birmingham, during which Professor Webster made an additional statement about the teeth. He reported that, "so far as the teeth are concerned, I reported that she had her wisdom teeth in the bottom jaw but none in the upper jaw, they had not erupted. I have subsequently had the skull 'X'-Rayed and found that none would have erupted even had she lived to a very old age. So far as dental attention is concerned, she has definitely had one extraction in the lower jaw. The tooth was extracted long before her death. She also had a carious upper molar but she has never had fillings or worn a dental plate. Further, I reported to you that I was rather of the opinion she had never had pyorrhoea but on further examination

70

of the lower jaw, I am of the opinion that she may have suffered from slight pyorrhoea of the gums. It may have given her a foul breath or dirty appearance of the teeth, but it may not. The only other point about teeth is that in the lower jaw there is some definite over-lapping of the incisors..." Significantly, he then refers to the upper jaw, stating that "...the upper front teeth tended to project rather more than normal."

Despite Professor Webster highlighting the upper teeth, this observation is not reported in the first request (made on 11th May) for investigators to engage with dentists. Furthermore, only an image of the lower jaw is provided. It was not until 17th May (No.96, item 45) that the full-frontal image was produced. However, the dentists were only requested to check their records for the extracted first right molar, in the lower jaw.

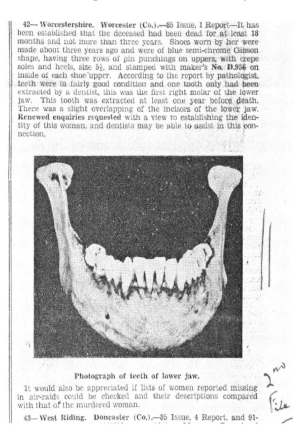

42— Worcestershire. Worcester (Co.).—85 Issue, 1 Report—It has been established that the deceased had been dead for at least 18 months and not more than three years. Shoes worn by her were made about three years ago and were of blue semi-chrome Gibson shape, having three rows of pin punchings on uppers, with crepe soles and heels, size 5½, and stamped with maker's No. D.956 on inside of each shoe upper. According to the report by pathologist, teeth were in fairly good condition and one tooth only had been extracted by a dentist, this was the first right molar of the lower jaw. This tooth was extracted at least one year before death. There was a slight overlapping of the incisors of the lower jaw. Renewed enquiries requested with a view to establishing the identity of this woman, and dentists may be able to assist in this connection.

Photograph of teeth of lower jaw.

It would also be appreciated if lists of women reported missing in air-raids could be checked and their descriptions compared with that of the murdered woman.

43— West Riding. Doncaster (Co.).—85 Issue, 4 Report, and 91-

Police Report No.92 item 42, dated 11th May, 1943.

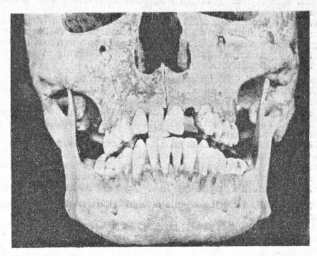

45—Worcestershire. Worcester (Co.).—84 Issue, 17 Report, 85-1, 87-26, and 92-42—

Photo of teeth of both upper and lower jaws of skeleton. The left laterel incisor of upper jaw is not shown on photograph as this fell out post-mortem and has not been recovered. Will Forces call the attention of dentists to the photograph, as deceased had one tooth, the first right molar of the lower jaw, extracted some time before death.

The Skull: The Professor notes that there were no marks of injury on the skull: all the soft tissue had gone, whilst a few hairs were still stuck to the top right-hand side of the skull. Inside the skull, there were considerable quantities of old blood, mainly on the right side. This indicated that the skull had lain on its right-hand side prior to being discovered—pooling the fluid and protecting the hair from the elements, animal and entomology activity.

The first of the bones, as well as the skull, arrived in the laboratory on the evening of 20th April. Dr Lund describes how Professor Webster identified to him some cloth 'firmly pressed into the skull' which he recovered and identified as being a remnant of the skirt.[77] This concurs with what the boys reported:

---

[77] Steve Punt (2015) radio interview.

they believed that during the process of jabbing at the skull, some cloth was pushed into the foramen magnum.

In the interview, Dr Lund indicates that this was the only piece of skirt recovered, which contradicts Professor Webster's account. He reports that at the crime scene, pressed over the lower jaw in the cavity of the mouth, he found part of the khaki-coloured dress.

The top of the skull was also used to estimate Bella's age using the sutures. Webster remarks that "they are plainly marked on the outside, and on the inside they are still plainly visible. These markings disappear in late middle life. The sagittal suture shows commencing obliteration when viewed from inside and this condition usually commences at the age of 25 years and closure may

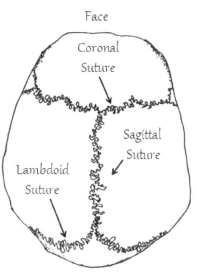

be quite marked at the age of 40 years. Hence, from the condition of the sutures this skull is quite definitely between 25 and 40 years."

The use of the sagittal suture for aging was well established in 1943, as was the need to use other anthropological calculators alongside one another. Today, most textbooks and other studies use the same study findings.[78] The exceptions[79] since the 1940s are an acknowledgement that closure of skull sutures occurs

---

[78] Todd TW, Lyon DW (1924) Endocranial suture closure, its progress and age relationship.

[79] Kumar et al., J Forensic Res 2012, 3:10: Fusion of Skull Vault Sutures in Relation to Age-A Cross Sectional Post-mortem Study conducted in 3rd, 4th & 5th Decades of Life.

earlier in males than females, whilst the commencement and closure range has increased with a revised period of twenty to fifty years.

He considers using the teeth for aging, although due to their 'irregular' condition, he suggests that no reliance for an age can be placed upon them; instead, he feels that referencing the sutures is of more importance.

The Hyoid Bone - The horseshoe-shaped bone found in the neck. At the crime scene, amongst the debris and below the lower jaw, the Professor recovered a small piece of thin, fragile bone which, in his opinion, was one of the cornua of a hyoid bone. The rest of the hyoid was missing, a loss he put down to the 'ravages of animals'. He notes ossification had not taken place between the body of the hyoid and cornu - a condition which he also believes places Bella under the age of forty. He indicates that the bone was free because it had not fused with the other bones. By 1952,[80] the pathology of fractures of the hyoid bone in death by strangulation became known. This, however is dependent on the nature and magnitude of force applied to the neck, the age of the victim, and the type of instrument (ligature or hands) used to strangle the victim.

The Sternum - Professor Webster notes that the sternum (breast bone) was present, except for the xiphisternum, and there was incomplete fusion between the manubrium and the body of the sternum. This fusion is another indicator of age; as the union of the xiphi with the body usually takes place at approximately forty years of age, the union of the manubrium and the body occurs at a later period. He notes that, "...the ossification of this bone is again notoriously irregular, and, though it would appear from the condition of the manubrium and body, that this woman was over 40, the fact that the xiphoid and the body have not united outweighs the former evidence with regards to this bone,

---

[80] Keith Simpson p.98.

and in my opinion, so far as the sternum is concerned, the balance of evidence is that again this woman was under 40."

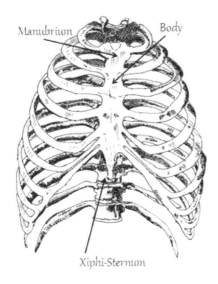

Pelvis - The pelvis was recovered in three parts: the sacrum, and the two separate hip or iliac bones. These had suffered considerably from the ravages of animals: small parts of them were missing. Judging theses bones, Professor Webster is of the opinion, "...that the sex characteristics of the pelvis are unquestionably female."

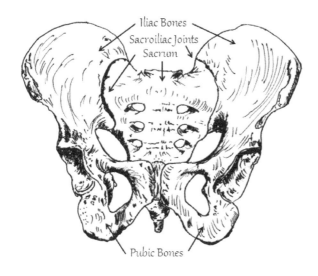

Highlighted in the autopsy report is a feature in the two hip bones, known as 'parturition scars', which were associated with previous childbirth. It is thought that during the process of childbirth, the ligaments tear on the pubic bones and sacroiliac joint, causing scars or pits. It is even claimed that the number of births could be estimated by the size and number of so-called 'parturition pits'.

Since the 1940s, studies have found scars on females who have never had children, with scar size and shape showing variation regardless of the number of children born. Scarring can be caused by activities such as horseback riding and habitual squatting. Professor Webster was aware of these limitations and does say that previous childbirth "is not conclusive."

Age is also a consideration in the pelvis: it was noted that the ilium and the rest of the bone was firmly united—a process (which the Professor indicates) takes place by the end of the twenty-fifth year. However, recent studies have shown fusion in women to have completed by the age of twenty-three.

Femur – Upper Leg: Both femur bones were recovered; they measured forty-one centimetres in length. The epiphysea had united at both the upper and lower ends—a condition usually completed by approximately the twenty-second year.

Fibulae and Tibiae – Lower Leg: Both fibulae were recovered from the tree; however, the left tibia was found some distance from the tree, whilst the right tibia was not recovered and is still missing. The left tibia was also incomplete, with the malleolus (bottom end) having been chewed away. Given its incomplete state, Professor Webster estimated that the longest measurement of this bone was thirty cm.

The autopsy statement, dated 23rd April (which provides the baseline for this chapter) was also used at the inquest on the 28th to inform both the police investigation and media briefs.

Professor Webster provides five conclusions about the victim: gender, age, height, cause and time of death. However, later, at the No.9 Regional Conference on 3rd May, he clarifies his earlier observations as referenced below.

1. He is in no doubt that it was a female skeleton due to the evident female characteristics in the pelvis and skull.

2. He is quite certain that 'Bella' was over twenty-five years of age but under forty; ascertained from the suture condition in the skull. He is of the opinion that she was some years under forty, putting her probable approximate age at thirty-five— that is to say thirty-five, plus or minus a few years.

He then clarifies that "...you can discard completely anyone under the age of 25. I am satisfied about that. This woman, unfortunately, has not undergone the usual routine joining up of her bones, but I am equally certain that the other limit is 40 years of age. Further, I gave as an estimate probably 35 years of age, but I cannot be definite as on the other two points, but my impression is that she is on the 40 side of 35 rather than on the 30 side of 35."

3. Using the 'Karl Pearson's formulae', he believes Bella was definitely under the average height for a woman, estimating her to be roughly sixty inches in height.[81]

Bone	Measurement
<u>Humeri</u>	Longest Diameter 28.2 cm.
Radius & Ulna	Radii measuring 19cm.
Femur	41cm. in length
Tibia	~30 cm.

He later clarifies that, "...the height of five feet which I gave to you is the height as she would appear when going about. I took into consideration her shoes. Actually she was about 4' 9 ½" to 4' 10 ½" and in her shoes would be about 5 feet."

---

[81] Pearson, Karl. (1931) Tables for statisticians and biometricians p.XXV.

4. Other than asphyxia resulting from the khaki-coloured skirt being forced into the mouth, the skeleton gave no unequivocal proof as to the cause of death.

He later clarifies that, "...with regard to the murder, as I said at the inquest you have no cause of death, no definite cause of death. The fact of the matter is this, that I found in this woman's mouth part of her clothing stuffed well in. If that was put in during life it could have caused asphyxia by suffocation."

5. Regarding the time of death, Professor Webster notes that once bones become completely stripped of the flesh, they may remain in a dried condition, similar to how they were found, for years. Hence, he was only willing to speculate on the minimum time the body would have lain where it was found. He states, "the flesh has completely gone from these bones, but, although the sutures of the skull were not closed, they have not fallen apart. Moreover, I found that there was considerable growth of the roots of this tree through the remainder of the clothing, and, taking into consideration all these factors, I am of the opinion that this body must have been there a minimum period of 18 months, but may have been there for a very considerably longer period."

He later clarifies, "with regard to the time of death, I prefer to give the minimum time; that is to say eighteen months. As I told Superintendent Inight that minimum does not by any means mean that I feel sure that death occurred 18 months ago. From the condition of the bones my own opinion is that she might have been there three years. I will not limit myself too much one way or another. Between 18 months and three years is the period I should say."

In addition to clarifying the five conclusions, he also elaborates on other issues. Regarding the teeth, he initially reported she had never had pyorrhoea. On further examination of the lower jaw, he was of the opinion that she may have suffered from slight pyorrhoea of the gums. This may have given her foul breath or made her teeth appear dirty, although it may not have.

Webster was asked if the bones gave a clue to her occupation. He concludes that she showed none of the changes associated with constant, hard agricultural work; there were no employments that necessitated using one side of her body more than another, nor was her work of a particularly hard nature, as there was no obvious excessive muscular development.

He apparently did not say at the inquest that the woman had ever given birth; however, he was clear to the investigators that, in his opinion, she had one pregnancy at least.

Professor Webster had considered facial reconstruction. He notes that there had only been one successful reconstruction of a face from a skeleton and that had been in the U.S.A. In that instance, it was known that the victim was an Italian; this, of course, helped considerably. He was concerned that the reconstruction might be misleading if he gave the woman (for example) a long nose when she had a short one. He concluded his observations by saying he was still considering the matter - there is nothing to indicate he ever continued with this option.

The next time anthropology was considered was reported in Detective Chief Inspector Nicholls's closure report, dated 13th July, 2005. Under the title 'Forensic Strategy', reference is made to the consideration of a Forensic Anthropologist, but again there is nothing to indicate it was undertaken. A freedom of information request for details of the forensic decision process yielded a negative response.

I felt that one of the few remaining ways of identifying Bella was through a facial depiction, and therefore I approached Professor Caroline Wilkinson (from Face Lab at Liverpool John Moores University) to ask for her help.

13
Facial Reconstruction

Prof Caroline Wilkinson and Sarah Shrimpton from Face Lab at Liverpool John Moores University were asked to produce a facial depiction based on the images of the human remains. Photographs were utilised to produce a 2D facial reconstruction, using Adobe Photoshop CC.

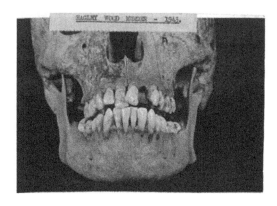

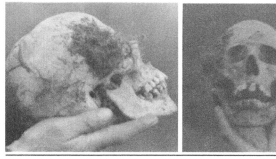

The hard tissue analysis suggested that the unknown remains were those of an adult female (most likely in her mid-30s according to the original pathology report). The skull was intact, and the mandible had been articulated with the cranium in one image.

The skull appeared to have moderate muscle attachments but mild supra-orbital ridges, a square-to-oval jawline, and an upright forehead; these latter details are consistent with a female, as suggested in previous accepted research. From the images, the skull showed an upright profile, a high, steepled nasal root, angular orbits, a sharp nasal margin and a depressed glabella, suggesting a Caucasoid-type ancestry. These details are consistent with an individual of Caucasoid ancestry, as suggested by previous accepted research. This also suggests origins from Europe, the Middle East or the Indian sub-continent. There were some indications of a sub-Saharan African type ancestry due to the mild prognathism and post-bregmatic depression; however, the overall shape and features of the skull were more consistent with a Caucasoid ancestry.

The skull morphological analysis suggested that the skull was moderately robust, with moderate muscle attachments but a more robust mandible shape with gonial flaring. The upper incisors were prominent, with some overlapping of the central incisors, producing a local overjet over the lower teeth and mild prognathism (forward protruding oral cavity). The images suggest that the anterior lacrimal crest and malar tubercle had slightly upturned eye fissures. The canine fossa was moderately deep and deeper nearer the palate, suggesting a soft naso-labial crease that is stronger around the mouth.

The nasal bones suggested a short nose with an upturned columella, flat alae and a pointed nasal tip. The vomer bone deviates slightly to the right, indicating that the nose would have also deviated to the right. The brow ridges and supraorbital margin suggested an arched eyebrow pattern.
A 2D facial reconstruction was produced following the Manchester method. Adobe Photoshop CC was used to map out lines of reference for the measurements of the features.

Facial features were imported from face photo databases and distorted to fit the skull following standards. Photoshop's mask, warp, liquify and resize tools were used to adjust the feature samples to fit the skull. The missing upper left second incisor

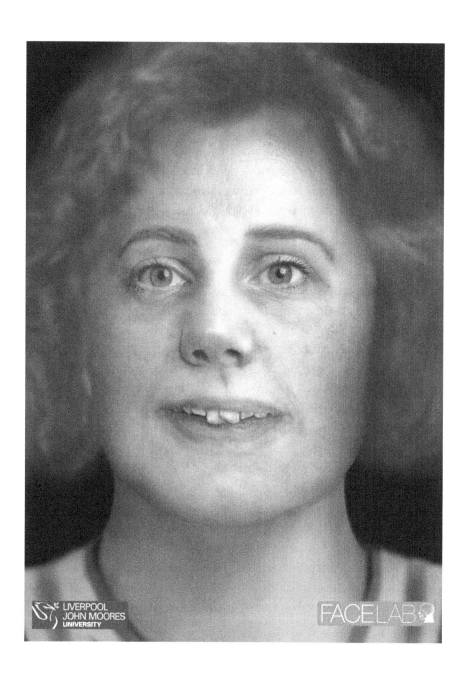

was remodelled by mirroring the upper right second incisor and rescaling and translating the tooth to fit the skull.

Clothing and hairstyle information was taken from Dr Lund's clothing report for the final image. The final depiction is presented as a grayscale image, with a pale skin tone textured according to the reported age and ancestry. It must be noted that this facial reconstruction is NOT an accurate portrait of the face of the person, but rather a representation of the face based on the available skull images. The images provided for facial reconstruction were of varying quality, size and angle. Inconsistencies between the depiction and the face of the person are, therefore, inevitable. However, this image was designed to represent the face of the person in relation to proportions and morphology.

14
The Origins of Bella

Whilst this book is about revisiting the crime scene, the name given to the mystery (and to this book) originated around a year after the discovery and is an element worth touching on.

Grafitti aabout the case started in Birmingham on 28th March, 1944, when Mr Wilfred L. White reported seeing, written in chalk on the walls adjoining White's on Pershore Street, **'HAGLEY WOOD BELLA'** and on the wall of Williamson's Upper Dean Street, **'WHO PUT BELLA DOWN THE WYCH ELM – HAGLEY WOOD'**.

A few days later, on 30th March, Mr James W. Rowley, reported[82] seeing on a cottage wall along Haden Hill, Old Hill in Halesowen, the caption, **'WHO PUT LUEBELLER IN THE WYCH ELM'**. All the writings appeared to be similar, and the Old Hill caption had the words Luebeller and Wych Elm underlined.

The wording was photographed at all locations, with samples of chalk recovered. On 5th April, they were submitted to the Forensic Science Laboratory (South Wales and Monmouthshire

---

[82] Insp Hughes, Old Hill, report dated 4th April, 1944.

area). Shortly afterwards, the laboratory reported that the inscriptions were by the same person and that the chalk was more or less similar[83].

The Birmingham Gazettee ran an article on the writings, which raised interest in the murder, as well as 'encoraging' a spate of copy cat messages. On 12th April, 1944, more writing appeared, this time on a wall which adjoined the premises of Messrs Walter Seamers and opposite the works of Messrs Laminated springs on Mucklows Hill, Halesowen. Detective Constable Lee of the Halesowen section produced the following note:

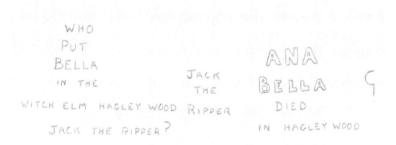

WHO PUT BELLA IN THE WITCH ELM HAGLEY WOOD
JACK THE RIPPER?
ANA BELLA DIED IN HAGLEY WOOD

On 15th April, Sergeant Skerratt and DI Williams travelled to view the writing for themselves but believed it was not the same as what they had seen before at Old Hill and Birmingham.

Things went quiet for a few months until 1st August, 1944, when Mr Ray was walking along Sun Passage (now Sun Street) in Wolverhampton (from Heath Town towards the railway station) when he saw on his right, underneath an archway, the caption,

---

[83] R Harrison, Director, Forensic Science Laboratory (South Wales and Monmouthshire area) report dated 12th April, 1944, Hagley Wood Murder. Ref: WRH/ML/C.2082.

'HAGLEY WOOD LUBELLA ADDRESS OPPOSITE THE ROSE AND CROWN HASBURY'.

This was followed, on 3rd August, by writing on a fence (or part of a gate) at Shelton Lane, opposite the Shelton Inn. The caption read, **'ADDRESS WAS OPPOSITE ROSE AND CROWN HASBURY HAGLEY WOOD LUBELLA'.**

Nearby, on a wall underneath the railway arch,[84] was the caption, **'HAGLEY WOOD LUBELLA WAS NO PROSS'.** Although officially reported on 3rd August, both had been seen there at least a fortnight earlier.

---

[84] DI Williams report, chalked writing on wall and fence at belle vale Halesowen, dated 4th August, 1944.

In October, another caption appeared on a wall in Oldbury, **'HAGLEY WOOD LUBELLA ADDRESS WAS 404 LOWER HASBURY HALESOWEN'**. Investigations were carried out at the address which was occupied by Mr and Mrs Allsopp. They had lived there for the last fifty-six years, meaning this inquiry led nowhere[85].

1944 saw the start of the messages, which continue to this day. It was in 1993 that the phrase **'WHO PUT BELLA IN THE WITCH ELM'** appeared on the Wychbury obelisk.

---

[85] DC 215 Lee, Halesowen Section report dated 31st October, 1944.

Date	Location	Caption
27/03/44	Williamsons, 19 Upper Dean Street Birmingham	Who put Bella down the Wytch-elm Hagley Wood
27/03/44	Haden Hill, Old Hill, Halesowen - possibley there before Xmas 1943	Who put LUE BELLER in the Wych Elm
30/03/44	Whites, Pershore Street Birmingham	HAGLEY WOOD BELLA
12/04/44	Mucklows Hill, Halesowen	WHO PUT BELLA IN THE WITCH ELM HAGLEY WOOD JACK THE RIPPER? ANA BELLA DIED IN HAGLEY WOOD
01/08/44	Sun Passage, Wolverhampton	HAGLEY WOOD LUBELLA ADDRESS OPPOSITE THE ROSE AND CROWN HASBURY
03/08/44	Under railway near Shelton Lane	HAGLEY WOOD LUBELLA WAS NO PROSS
03/08/44	Fence at Shelton Lane	ADDRESS WAS OPPOSITE ROSE AND CROWN HASBURY HAGLEY WOOD LUBELLA

15
Looking Forward

My journey started with an article in the local newspaper advertising an up-and-coming documentary about 'Bella'; which in turn took me and my father to the top of Wychbury Hill to see some graffiti - I would never have guessed that it would have resulted in a book.

It has been a rewarding process, but not without challenges especially with my school work and I probably spent too much time researching and writing and not enough time revising for exams. I am indebted to a very large number of people; official bodies, private organisations and individuals who we contacted for advice and guidance – everyone has been so helpful and supportive, and without their assistance and encouragement I would never have started or finished.

I could not end without acknowledging the immeasurable assistance given to me by my father who not only encouraged me throughout but took me on numerous trips to visit archives, helped with my writing, the gathering of research material and for making the contacts and introductions to so many people. A special thanks to Ann Swaby, her help in gathering the research material was vital, Professor Caroline Wilkinson and Sarah Shrimpton from the Face Lab at Liverpool John Moores University for bringing Bella to life and Rik Rawling for his amazing illustrations.

This book is not, however, the definitive edition: I've had access to many official documents which were not available to previous authors; who knows what the future holds, other personal accounts, recovered reports and photographs will undoubtedly emerge. Forensic science students may choose to research and develop my theories further - especially the clothing, decomposition and an archaeological survey. This means that new chapters can and will be written, additions and amendments will be made, and Bella's story made richer for them – I embrace that thought and wish whoever takes that challenge forward in the future enjoys the experience as much as I have?

The greatest mystery so far to me is what category of person I am; an amateur detective, investigative researcher, or just an obsessionist and theorists. I wanted to 'shake the kaleidoscope', to add a new perspective and to shed light on other possibilities and I sincerely hope I have achieved that?

Alex Merrill January 2018

Acknowledgements and Freedom Of Information (FOI) requests:

The National Archives

Worcestershire Archives and Archaeology - Ref: 010:18 Acc No. 14908; Police files relating to the Hagley Wood

The Library of Birmingham; Archive and Collection - Ref: MS4724, Home Office: Forensic Science Laboratory, Birmingham

Warwickshire & West Mercia Police FOI No: 8269

West Midlands Police FOI No: 2653/17 & 7535/17

Home Office FOI No. 45997

British Medical Council FOI No. F17/9192/SW

G U Williams LLB, HM Senior Coroner for Worcestershire

SATRA Technology – shoe enquiry.

Reference books/media:

1. William Boyd (1932) A Text-Book of Pathology
2. Arthur Ward (1948) Stuff and Silk.
3. Keith Simpson (1952) Forensic Medicine 2nd Ed.
4. Percy Sillitoe (1955) Cloak Without Dagger.
5. J.B. Firth (1960) A Scientist Turns To Crime.
6. Rupert Furneaux (1962) Famous Criminal Cases *7*.
7. Kenneth Ullyett (1963) Crime Out Of Hand.
8. Donald McCormick (1969) Murder by Witchcraft a Study of the Lower Quinton and Hagley Wood Murders.
9. A.K. Mant (1973), 'A survey of forensic pathology in England since 1945', Journal of the Forensic Science Society.
10. DG Browne & T Tullett (1981) Bernard Spilsbury, His Life And Cases.
11. Norman Vincent Ambage (1987) The Origins and Development of the Home Office Forensic Science Service, 1931-1967.
12. E. Giles & P.H. Vallandigham (1991) Height Estimation from Foot and Shoe Print Length, Journal of Forensic Sciences, Vol. 36, No. 4, July 1991, pp. 1134-1151.
13. Jennifer Ward (1993) Origins and development of forensic medicine and forensic science in England 1823-1946.
14. Bernard Knight (1993) Simpson's Forensic Medicine 10Ed.
15. Bob Pooler (2002) from Fruit Trees To Furnaces: A history of the Worcestershire Constabulary.
16. Brian Lane (2004) Chronicle of murder: a dark and bloody history of our age.
17. Matthew Gull (2005) Inside Out, BBC West Midlands, broadcasted 9th September 2005 – Murder Mystery.
18. John Mervyn Pugh (2005) Execution, One Man's Life And Death.
19. Joyce M Coley (2007) Bella: An Unsolved Murder.
20. Anne Bradford (2008) Foul Deeds & Suspicious Deaths around Worcester.
21. Nicola Sly (2009) Worcestershire Murders.
22. Paul Newman (2009) Under The Shadow of Meon Hill.

23. Michael Posner (2009) Bristol Murders.
24. K Layborn & D Taylor (2011) Policing in England and Wales, 1918-39: The Fed, Flying Squads and Forensics.
25. S.P. Jitender, C.M. Mahesh, R. Y, K.S. Girish (2013) Stature Estimation from the Dimensions of Foot in Females Antrocom Online Journal of Anthropology 2013, vol. 9, pp 237-241.
26. Andrew Sparke (2014) Bella in the Wych Elm: In Search of a Wartime Mystery
27. Andy Williams (2014) Forensic Criminology
28. Steve Punt (2015) Punt PI – broadcasted 6th Aug, BBC Radio 4 Who Put Bella in The Wych Elm?
29. Jayne Harris (2017) The Untold Story, Documentary.
30. Newspapers
    a. Birmingham Daily Gazette
    b. Birmingham Daily Post
    c. Birmingham Mail
    d. Birmingham Post And Journal
    e. Express And Star
    f. Glasgow Times
    g. South Wales Echo
    h. University of Birmingham Gazette
    i. Wolverhampton Express & Star

West Midlands Forensic Science Laboratory
Director James M. Webster, M.A., B.Sc., M.B.Ch.B, F.R.C.S. (Ed.)
Telephone Colmore 4170
Newton Street, Birmingham, 4
23rd April, 1943
[Stamped: Worcestershire Constabulary - Crime Investigation Department - 23 APR 1943 - Castle Street Worcester]

HUMAN REMAINS FOUND IN A HOLLOW TREE IN HAGLEY WOOD ON THE MAIN BIRMINGHAM-KIDDERMINSTER ROAD.

On 20th April, 1943, at about 6.30 p.m., in company with officers of the Worcestershire County police Force, and with other assistance I recovered from the hollow bole of the stum of an elm tree in Hagley Wood on the main Birmingham - Kidderminster Road certain human remains and garments. These remains consisted of a disarticulated skeleton. The skeleton was incomplete and at the time I recovered a human tibia or shin bone about 12 yards from the tree.

On the 22nd instant I received from the Worcestershire Constabulary a left pelvic bone, a right femur, and a right fibula. The combined bones make up a human skeleton, and they are parts of one body and one body only. The skeleton is incomplete and is minus the right tibia or shin bone, part of the hyoid bone, a patella, and some of the small bones of the hands and feet.

Skull

The skull was in two parts, consisting of the head, which lay exposed on the floor of the tree bole, and the lower jaw, which was in line with the disarticulated vertebrae under the overhanging entrance to the hollow bole. This skull is undoubtedly human and is that of a female.

Upper Jaw.

In the upper jaw the two central incisors, the left lateral incisor, and the second right molar are missing. From examination of the sockets, however, these had dropped out post-mortem and were present in the head at the time of this woman's death. The teeth which remain are in good condition except that the second left premolar is carious. There is no evidence of this person having suffered from pyorrhoea. Neither of the third molars in the upper jaw has erupted. The teeth, moreover, are clean.

There are no marks of injury on the skull, and all the soft tissue has gone. A few hairs were still adherent to the top of the skull. The inside of the skull shows a considerable quantity of old blood on the right side. This, however, is so decomposed that it is impossible to say if this blood was shed ante-mortem or was due to post-mortem postural changes. It is true that this old blood is situated over the right middle meningeal artery, but, in the absence of any injury to the skill, it is reasonable to suppose that this did not come from the middle that this did not come from the middle meningeal artery during life. The sutures of the skull are plainly marked on the outside, and on the inside they are still plainly visible. These markings disappear in late middle life. The sagittal suture shows commencing obliteration when viewed from inside, and this condition usually commences at the age of 25 years and closure may be quite marked at the age of 40 years. Hence, from the condition of the sutures the age of this skull is quite definitely between 25 and 40 years.

There is a slight anomaly with regard to the dentition in the upper jaw in that the third molars, which are unerupted in this case, usually erupt in females at the age of between 18 and 1(*overwritten* 2)4 years, but the eruption of third molars is notoriously irregular. Hence, no reliance as to age can be placed upon the teeth, and they are infinitely less important from the point of view of age than the sutures.

There is a little bloodstaining all over this skull on the outside.

Lower Jaw.

In the lower jaw the dentition has been complete, the third molars having erupted. The teeth are in fiarly good condition, but the first left molar is extremely carious, and the first right molar had been extracted a considerable time before death, since the socket had had time to heal completely. There is nothing

95

particularly distinctive about the teeth except for the fact that there is slight overlapping of the incisors. The best way, I consider, of describing the incisor teeth is that there would have been a noticeable irregularity of the incisors. Further, with regard to the lower jaw, this, when found by me, was in line with the spine.

Tightly pressed over the lower jaw in the cavity of the mouth I found part of the khaki or mustard coloured dress which the deceased was wearing at the time of death. So far as this thrust over the teeth margin and so firmly adherent to the teeth was this part of the apparel that I do not consider it likely – I cannot say impossible – that this came into the mouth accidentally after death. It appears much more probable that this had been forced into the mouth prior to death, and, if so, this would have been capable of causing death from asphyxia.

Clavicles. The two clavicles are present, and these show no sign of disease or injury, recent or old.

Hyoid Bone.

I recovered from the debris below the lower jaw a small piece of thin fragile bone which in my opinion constitutes one of the cornua of a human hyoid bone. The rest of the hyoid was missing, and this might well be accounted for by the ravages of animals. It is obvious from this portion of the hyoid that ossification had not taken place between the body of the hyoid and cornua – a condition which again places this woman under the age of 40.

Scapulae.

Both scapulae are present, but neither of these bones shows any distinctive feature.

Sternum.

The sternum is present except the xiphi sternum, and there is incomplete fusion between the manubrium and the body of the sternum. Whilst it is true that the union of the xiphoid to the body usually takes place at about 40 years of age, and the union of the manubrium and the body at a much later period, the ossification of this bone is again notoriously irregular, and, though it would appear from the condition of the manubrium and body, that this woman was over 40, the fact that the xiphoid and the body have not united outweighs the former evidence with regards to this bone, and in my opinion, so far as the sternum is concerned, the balance of evidence is that again this woman was under 40.

Humeri.

The two humeri are present and measured in the longest diameter 28.2 cm. Here again there is no distinctive feature, the bones showing neither injury nor disease. All the epiphyses have joined up.

Radii and Ulnae.

The bones of the forearm, namely, the radius and ulna, are present on both sides, the radii measuring 19cm. Again there is no distinctive feature, all the epiphyses have joined up.

Spine and Ribs.

The complete spine and ribs are present. None of these shows injury or ante-mortem abnormality. Further, there are none of the changes due to age on the spine and there is no lipping or evidence of arthritis. The curvatures of the spine are normal.

Pelvis.

The pelvis is in three parts, namely, the sacrum, and the two separate hip or iliac bones. The sex characteristics of the pelvis are unquestionably female. Both pelvic bones have suffered considerably from the ravages of animals, and small parts of them are missing. There is one feature in the two hip bones, namely, the well-marked condition of the pre-auricular sulcus, which is frequently associated with previous childbirth, but this is not conclusive. The epiphysis between the crest of the ilium and the rest of the bone is firmly united – a process which takes place by the end of the 25th year.

Femora.

The two femora are present and measure 41cm. In length. The epiphysea have united at both the upper and lower ends – a condition usually completed by about the 22nd year. The trabeculae of bone at the lower end of the femur are not quite continuous across the line of the epiphysis, again showing that this person had not reached advanced age. These bones again show no distinctive feature.

Fibulae and Tibiae.

Both fibulae are present and again show no distinctive features, the epiphyses being united. The right tibia is missing, but the left tibia, which was found at some distance from the tree, is present, though incomplete, the maleolus having been chewed away. The estimated longest measurement of this bone is 30 cm.

Foot Bones.

Most of the small bones of the feet are present. There is nothing distinctive about these, and examination of the two first metatarsals gives no indication that this woman had suffered from any distinctive deformity such as bunions – a conclusion which is borne out by an examination of her shoes.

CONCLUSIONS.

The following are my conclusions with regard to the skeleton.

Sex.

There can be no doubt that this is a female skeleton. The female characteristics are so evident in the pelvis and skull as to leave one in no dubiety about this.

Age.

One can be quite certain that this woman was over 25 years of age and under 40. From the condition of the sutures of the skull, this woman was in my opinion some years under 40, and I would put her probable approximate age as 35, that is to say 35 either plus or minus a few years.

Stature.

Using Karl Pearson's formulae, I am of opinion that this was a woman definitely under average height, and my estimates with these formulae place her at about 60 inches in height.

Cause of Death.

There remain only bones from this body, and there are many causes of death in accident, suicide and murder which do not affect the bony skeleton, there is no unequivocal proof in the skeleton as to the cause of death, but, as I have indicated the position of the mustard or khaki coloured skirt forced into the mouth as I found it, does not appear to me to be likely to be accidental, and could most certainly, if pushed into the mouth during life, have caused death from asphyxia.

Accident, Suicide, or Murder.

There is no indication in the skeleton or in the clothing as to which of these conditions played a part in this woman's death. Consideration, however, of the bole of the tree in which this skeleton was found leads me to the conclusion that this was much more likely to be murder than the other two propositions. The entrance to this tree was extremely narrow and would have caused not merely inconvenience, but actual injury if even a small woman of this nature should have forced herself into the tree. Further, I do not think that this was a likely position for committing suicide. Accident can, I think, be entirely ruled out. The tree, however, afforded an excellent concealment for murder. From the position of the skeleton in the bole of the tree. I am of opinion that this woman was pushed in feet first. Moreover, she could only have been pushed in conveniently either before rigor mortis set in or after rigor mortis had passed off. If the body had been kept until rigor mortis had passed off, putrefaction would have commenced, and it is extremely unlikely that the murderer would have kept the body until it had got into this condition. Hence i am of opinion that this body was pushed into the tree before rigor mortis had set in. This being so, it is likely that the murder as committed in near vicinity to the tree, or, if committed at a distance, the murderer must have had a conveyance to enable him to get the body to the tree before rigor mortis set in.

Time of Death.

With regard to the time of death, I must point out that once bones become completely stripped of the flesh, they may remain in a dried condition similar to that we found in this case, for years. Hence it is only possible to give a minimum time for a body to have lain where it was found. The flesh has completely gone from these bones, but, although the sutures of the skull re not closed, they have not fallen apart. Moreover, I found that there was considerable growth of the roots of this tree through the remainder of the clothing, and, taking into consideration all these factors, i am of the opinion that this body must have been there a minimum period of 18 months, but may have been there for a very considerably longer period.

Shoes.

It would appear probable that the pair of shoes recovered one from the bole of the tree, and the other at some distance, are connected with this body. These shoes are black shoes, size 51/2, and from the information which I obtained, are probably made by Waterfoot Company, Lancashire. Inspector Williams, however, following his visit to Northampton, has considerably more information with regard to these shoes, and this seems to me a likely line to follow up.

Description of the Deceased.

Combining my own and Dr. Lund's observations, it appears to me that a very likely description of the deceased would be:

A woman aged between 25 and 40 years, most probably round about 35 years of age, 5ft. In height, with light ('mousy') brown hair; no undue prominence of the teeth, but noticeable irregularity of the front teeth in the lower jaw; clad in a dark blue and light khaki or mustard coloured striped knitted woollen cardigan with cloth covered buttons and a belt of a slightly brighter shade of blue than the blue stripes in the cardigan itself, a light khaki or mustard coloured woollen skirt with a side zip fastener, a peach-coloured taffeta rayon underskirt, navy blue interlock cotton knickers, corsets, and black crepe-soled shoes. The above person has been missing for at least 18 months. She was wearing a rolled gold enamelled ring.

James M Webster
Professor of forensic medicine and Toxicology,
University of Birmingham.

Document 2

Statement: Dr John Lund - Staff Biologist – Dated 23rd April 1943

Clothing examination, 21st April 1943:

Much of the material was in an advanced state of decomposition and in no case has it been possible to produce more than part of a garment. Excluding the shoes, which are the subject of a special enquiry there were portions of 5 garments present.

Portions of a pair of navy blue interlock cotton knickers. This is a cheap type of knicker.

Artificial silk taffeta material, such as is used to line coats and costumes. This material is sometimes made up into very cheap underskirts or taken from coats and made up in the home. Although this material seems somewhat long for a woman of 5 feet., and although I have been able to find any trace of shoulder straps, I am of the opinion that this is part of an underskirt and that in all probability the garment was home-made. If it was the lining of a coat, then every trace of that coat has disappeared, which, in view of the state of preservation of the other garments, is most likely. The original colour of this garment was probably peach or, less likely, pink.

Portions of the metal stays, metal front and suspenders of a corset. Apart from a very small fragment of material attached to the metal front, the fabric has rotted away, and hence it is very difficult to deduce much as to its quality. The metal portions are, however, identical with those used in the "wrap-round" type of corset now sold for about 8s. To 10s. And I think that is more likely to have been this kind of corset than the heavy old-fashioned type.

Portion of a good-class all wool garment which is almost certainly a skirt with a side metal zip fastening. The original colour of this was probably mustard or pale khaki, perhaps with a tinge of beige.

A knitted woollen cardigan with alternating pale khaki or mustard coloured (presumably to match the skirt) and dark blue stripes. This had cloth-covered buttons and a knitted wool belt of a somewhat brighter blue than that of the cardigan itself. The metal portion of a belt buckle is also present; there is no cloth attached to this but it is extremely unlikely that it was not covered. There is no sign of any sleeves to this garment, but this type of cardigan commonly has long sleeves.

There was no sign of any stockings, and therefore, as the case of the coat, I am of the opinion that there were none.

Presuming that this is all the clothing the woman was wearing, it is clear that she was lightly dressed for outdoors and that the general quality of the garments was poor.

There was an extensive growth of tree roots into the pieces of clothing. From this fact and the state of disintegration of the garments, it is my opinion that they have been in the tree for at least 18 months.

There was a large quantity of head hair present, all of it is very brittle and rotted state. It is impossible to tell what kind of hair style this woman affected, but there is no sign of permanent waving. There is a <u>little</u> natural waving. The hair has not been dyed or bleached. It is also impossible to be accurate as to the length of the hair. I have found a few hairs 7 inches long. The most I can say is that it was neither very short nor very long. There were a few grey hairs, and the general colour was a light ('mousy') brown.

Summary

From this examination, the following general conclusions may reasonably be inferred.

This woman had a good crop of light ('mousy) brown hair.

She was wearing a dark blue and light khaki or mustard coloured woollen cardigan with cloth-covered buttons a belt of a slightly brighter shade of blue the blue stripes in the cardigan itself; a light khaki or mustard coloured woollen cloth skirt with a side zip fastener; corsets; and dark blue crepe-soled shoes.

The clothing is of poor quality.

The presence of corsets suggests that this was not a young girl.

This amount of clothing for outdoors suggests that it was summer wear.

The condition of the hair and clothing and the mat of roots intertwined with the latter point to their having been in the tree for at least 18 months.

Document 3

Minutes of No.9 Regional Conference held at Birmingham on 3rd May 1943

Pages -6-8- Forensic Report

Professor J.M. Webster, M.A, B,Sc,.M.B.Ch.B.,F.R.C.S.(Ed), Professor of Forensic Medicine & Toxicology at Birmingham University, Director, West Midland Forensic Science Laboratory; Superintendent J.J. Hollyhead (Worcestershire); Det. Supt. F. Richardson (Birmingham) and Det. Inspr. T. Williams (Worcestershire), the facts so far known to the police in what has been termed the "Hagley Wood Skeleton".

Professor Webster, continued the Chairman, had worked very hard on the case, and the result of his examination of the remains was that the inquest verdict was one of murder against some person or persons unknown.

The wood is well known to many people and the tree in which the body was hidden was the best and indeed the only place where a body could be hidden in the wood. The use of such a place of concealment would appear to indicate local knowledge.

The Chairman, continuing, said there was certain evidence about the tooth, a ring and two shoes which were found and in respect of which there was a helpful turn. Enquiry into missing persons had not produced any good result.

Professor Webster said, "To commence with, one or two general things about the woman in regard to establishing her identity. Firstly, I want to make perfectly clear that the height of five feet which I gave to you is the height as she would appear when going about. I took into consideration her shoes. Actually she was about 4' 9 ½" to 4' 10 ½" and in her shoes would be about 5 feet.

Secondly, you can discard completely anyone under the age of 25. I am satisfied about that. This woman, unfortunately, has not undergone the usual routine joining up of her bones, but I am equally certain that the other limit is 40 years of age.

Further, I gave as an estimate probably 35 years of age, but I cannot be definite as on the other two points, but my impression is that she is on the 40 side of 35 rather than on the 30 side of 35. In addition to being a small woman, she had brown mousy hair; I cannot tell you if this was bobbed or waved and so on, for the very simple reason that whilst it looks a long complete mass, it consists of a number of broken pieces due to the action of the weather.

So far as the teeth are concerned, I reported that she had her wisdom teeth in the bottom jaw but none in the upper jaw, they had not erupted. I have subsequently had the skull 'X'-Rayed and found that none would have erupted even had she lived to a very old age. So far as dental attention is concerned, she has definitely had one extraction in the lower jaw. The tooth was extracted long before her death. She also had a carious upper molar but she has never had fillings or worn a dental plate. Further, I reported to you that I was rather of the opinion she had never had pyorrhoea but on further examination of the lower jaw, I am of the opinion that she may have suffered from slight pyorrhoea of the gums. It may have given her a foul breath or dirty appearance of the teeth, but it may not. The only other point about teeth is that in the lower jaw there is some definite over-lapping of the incisors and the upper front teeth tended to project rather more than normal.

Further, this woman has never had medical attention for ear trouble or sinus trouble, that is the cavities around the nose.

With regard to her status in life, from her clothing this woman is obviously not in the "higher flight" nor is she a ragamuffin. She is, moreover, a type of person who may have been rather neglectful as to her appearance and habits. This carious tooth which she had caused her considerable pain and must have given her a nasty taste in the mouth.

I do not think I can help much as to occupation except in the negative sense. She is perfectly symmetrical and shows none of the changes in her bones associated with constant hard agricultural work.

It is quite obvious that this woman's work, whatever it was, did not necessitate using one side of her body more than another, and thirdly her work was not of a particularly hard nature. There was obviously no excessive muscular development.

As I indicated in my report, there is a certain thing in this woman's skeleton that prevented me in the witness box from saying that this woman had had children. There is, however, one condition which points that she had one pregnancy at least.

With regard to the time of death, I prefer to give the minimum time; that is to say eighteen months. As I told Superintendent Inight that minimum does not by any means mean that I feel sure that death occurred 18 months ago. From the condition of the bones my own opinion is that she might have been there three years. I will not limit myself too much one way or another. Between 18 months and three years is the period I should say.

Now, with regard to the murder, as I said at the inquest you have no cause of death, no definite cause of death. The fact of the matter is this, that I found in this woman's mouth part of her clothing stuffed well in. If that was put in during life it could have caused asphyxia by suffocation.

The hollow tree had an upper aperture of 24 inches, funnel shaped, with an aperture of 17 inches lower down. I cannot imagine a woman accidently slipping in there, neither do I think it reasonable for a woman to crawl into that place to commit suicide. The aperture was narrow and the surface rugged and she would have caused herself damage to get in. It was an excellent place for the concealment of a murder and I think it indicates local knowledge.

From the position of the bones, the woman was not lying flat down but in a semi-reclining position. When the head rotted of and dropped down then the rest of the trunk dropped down. She must have been put in before rigor mortis or after it passed off. I will take the last condition first. If she was placed in afterwards, she must have been kept somewhere until she started to putrefy. This is very doubtful especially as she was dressed in full outdoor clothes. The other proposition is that she was put in before rigor mortis set in. She would either be killed close to the spot or she was murdered in the near vicinity so that it was possible to convey her to that spot before rigor mortis set in.

There is not much more about the skeleton itself that I can tell you except that it is one of the weaknesses of medical science that there are so many causes of death which leave no effect on the skeleton.

In such cases you have depredation caused not only by the weather but also by vermin.

Coming to the clothing, to a great extent I am indebted to Special Constable Goldfar in this matter. This woman had little clothing on. She had, first of all, close to the bones this so-called slip. (Here the Professor exhibited a piece of discoloured silky material). Regarding this, I think it was probably cut from a coat lining. It was, at least, a home –made slip and most of it gone. We have only a large piece from the back. It is cheap material and the interesting thing about it is that if it had been worn by the woman without a tuck, it would have shown under the skirt. Her corsets or corselets would however, have the effect of pulling the slip under the hem of the skirt. Det. Inspr. Williams has suggested that it might be part of a nightdress worn by the woman under her clothing at the time of an air raid.

The cardigan was of quite a good material and is of the ribbed variety. It is a rib of 5 ribs in one inch navy and 3 rids making up half an inch in mustard or khaki colour. The buttons are cloth-covered. There was a belt of slightly brighter shade of blue than the blue stripes in the cardigan.

The corset or corselet is definitely not old-fashion. I is a sort of corselet which fastens in front and has one or two stays to support it. It is a corselet rather than a corset.

There was no trace of stockings whatsoever. So far as weathering is concerned, while a great deal of the stockings might have gone, you would have had surviving some of the cotton. I am satisfied that she was not wearing stockings at the time".

A drawing of the cardigan was then exhibited and a reproduction of the slip; also a sample of blue locknit knickers as worn by the deceased. A mustard coloured skirt such as the woman wore was also exhibited. The original slip had been hemmed at the top and bottom by hand and was apparently home-made and had been dark peach or fawn – the Professor favoured fawn colour.

Sgt. Gwilliam (Wolverhampton) asked if it would be possible to have a photograph of a woman approximating that of the victim circulated who could be wearing the reproduced clothing.

Professor Webster pointed out that it was not possible to tell whether the woman was fat or thin.

The Chairman commented on the difficulty of securing coloured prints.

Professor Webster said he was considering writing away on this matter. There had only been one successful reconstruction of a face from a skeleton and that had been in the U.S.A. in that instance, it was known that the victim was an Italian, which of course helped considerably. If, for instance, he gave the woman a long nose it might be entirely misleading. He concluded his observations by saying he was still considering the matter.

In answer to a question whether one leg was longer than the other the Professor said that she was perfectly symmetrical. He had examined the acetabulums and they again were symmetrical. There were no changes there and from that, he learned there was no limp.

Sgt. Skerratt (Worcestershire) then dealt with the scene of the crime. He said the wood in which the body was found was thick with undergrowth and the tree 35 to 40 paces inside the wood from a lane. The main Birmingham – Kidderminster Road is 630 yards away.

Inspector Williams then dealt with his investigation into the case, particularly in connection with the shoes. The initial enquires were made at Northampton. He continued, "From Northampton the enquiry led to Bacup in Lancashire where this particular type of shoe is often made. It was thought there that the shoes were made by a firm al Leicester. All these enquiries had as their basis the number found inside the shoes, No.D.956. with regard to the number, various opinions were expressed as to whether it was the manufacturer's number or the number that identified it with a particular retailer. It is of interest to note that D.956 identified the shoes with the makers.

At Leicester the police were extremely helpful and I saw several directors and men in authority who had great experience in the shoe trade, and several expressed the opinion that they were made in Sileby, Leics. I was directed to a man who might possibly be able to tell me who made the shoes. This man, William Markham of 107, Beaumanor Road, Leicester, who is employed by Messrs. Greenlees Limited, East Oak Road, Leicester (Managing Director, Mr Lowe), and who is able to identify shoes made anywhere in England, told me there was a 75% chance that they were made by Brays of Sileby.

Brays of Sileby immediately identified them as their own shoes. I saw the manufacturer of the shoes and, with his assistance, it was established that this type of shoe had been supplied to four firms in all. They were first manufactured in April, 1940.

Document 4

Regarding Alleged Murder at Hagley Wood, deceased unknown:
19th April 1943

Commissioned by: Detective Chief Superintendent T. Albutt
Author: Detective Chief Inspector I Nicholls
Report Date: 13 July 2005

Introduction
The purpose of this document is to record the review of the
above file which pertains to the investigation surrounding the
recovery of the remains of a female from within the naturally
hollowed-out trunk of an elm tree located within Hagley Wood
adjacent to the main Birmingham to Kidderminster Road. This
road is now designated as this A456. The remains were first
reported on 19 April 1943. It was estimated that the body had
been so located for a period of not less than eighteen months.
When recovered the skeleton was disarticulated and certain
bones were missing. The nature of the bones missing would
induce a presumption that the absence was as a result of wildlife
intervention rather than being removed at the time of or
immediately after death. It was assessed that the individual has
entered the cavity feet first, and the probability of this occurring
willingly or intentionally was remote thus it was determined that
this matter was an offence of murder.
It is, I contend, most certainty an unexplained death however in
the absence of a specific cause of death or indeed any identified
injuries which indicate the individual was subjected to trauma,
that to make the leap to a murder is questionable. However, in
line with the current standards contained within the National
Crime Recording Standards   (Revised April 2004) specifically
the 'Balance of Probability' test, the balance is that the individual
was subjected to unlawful actions, which lead directly or
indirectly to her death

Executive Summary

Incident occurred at the height of Axis bombing of the West Midlands conurbation

The deceased has yet to be identified

Investigation centred on the identification of the diseased

Final resting-place still unknown

Investigation skewed by false reports

No further witnesses identified

Forensic opportunities examined however no advantages identified

Two potential suspects were identified as a result of information in 1953, one of whom was dead, the other remains untraced.

Investigation

The investigation of the offence centred primarily on the identification of the deceased, and through that process identifying any person who may have been involved in the death.

The identification phase centred upon the shoes retrieved from the scene, circulations appertaining to the deceased, and examination of missing persons allegedly missing.

To contextualise the event occurred at a time when considerable bombing by Axis forces was occurring within the Birmingham/Wolverhampton/Coventry conurbation, and thus it was considerably more common for persons to be transient and obviously death without record was a more frequent occurrence. During the course of the investigation a number of factors caused a skewing of the resources involved.

The first issue, which took up considerable effort, was the series of chalked messages upon walls throughout the West Midlands conurbation from Wolverhampton, into the Black Country and also into the city centre of Birmingham. The chalking's were undertaken over a protracted period of time. The reason for and also the author(s) of the chalking's were not established despite considerable investment.

Additionally considerable effort was expended attempting to identify the whereabouts of a Mary Wenman/Lee/Beaver, a traveller who at one time resided close to the location where the cadaver was recovered A soldier HEYWOOD, who was formerly having a relationship with the woman and sought to re-establish the relationship, initiated this. By a number of guises he used the Police to initiate an investigation to ascertain her whereabouts. The reality of the situation came to light and HEYWOOD subsequently admitted the details.

Bella TONKS was raised as a possibility following a media circulation The name 'Bella' was seemingly derived from the chalk writings on the walls throughout the West Midlands conurbation and as such the link to the enquiry was questionable. That said, the individual Bella Tonks was identified as living under her maiden name in Heath Hays.

Ann FORREST a traveller, was identified as having lived close to the deposition site, and was raised as potentially the deceased as a result of this. Enquiries traced FORREST in April 1944 as being alive and well.

Bella BEECH was draw to the inquiry's attention following her disappearance from bombed premises in West Ealing London. She had left the bombed premises to live in the Birmingham area, and contact had ceased. Enquiries traced this woman to a hospital in the London area where she was working as a nurse.

Bella LUER was a woman who moved from London to undertake factory work. The contact chain with persons in London was broken and thus she was raised as a possibility as being the deceased. Again the major factor was the term 'Bella'. Enquiries traced a Bella Luer as being a resident al Goring On Thames, however this individual was not definitely linked to the Bella Luer who was formerly resident in the Stamford Hill area of London.

Violet GOODE was a female who had been invoked in a relationship with Thomas Henry Truman resulting in his relationship with his wife Gladys Truman failing.

Subsequently Truman returned to his wife and a spurious assertion was made that GOODE had been killed to make way for this return. GOODE was identified as being alive and well, working and living in Stourbridge.

Lines of Enquiry Not Finalised

Dinah CURLEY aka O'GRADY

This line of enquiry commenced with the report of the above named person being missing by a woman, the recorded details of whom were Mrs M Lavin 56 Stanley Street, Manchester. This report prompted enquiries to trace both CURLEY and the reporter LAVIN. The thrust of the latter was following a labourer called Jack (John Edward) Lavin.

Document 112 outlines page two of details of a number of persons reported missing for the time appropriate to the belived death, provides a number of persons albeit there is no reference to investigation into the circumstances of their disappearance.

From the information supplied there is insufficient to identify whether CURLEY aka O'Grady in fact existed. Enquiries to trace the person M LAVIN failed to do so however there were a number of coincidences with the labourer Jack LAVIN. His wife was Mrs Mary LAVIN nee DOWLING. Their home was 40 Lawrence Street, Stockport, Manchester. The reporter of the missing person allegedly resided at 56 Stanley Street, Cheetham, Manchester however she moved in about 1941 to an address in 32 Robert Street, Cheetham Manchester with a family called Lynch. The LYNCH family subsequently removed to an address in Haverfordwest. Jack Lavin was employed on a contract in the St. David's area of west Wales, residing at an address on the Fishguard to Haverfordwest Road. Whilst there he was joined by his wife Mary.

Enquiries in the Haverfordwest area for the reporter LAVIN identified an address of 73 Belle Vue Terrace Haverfordwest until 30 March 1943 from where she removed to an address of 9 Claremont, Ripon, Yorkshire. The LYNCH family removed six months earlier to an address in Kettering, Northamptonshire Jack LAVIN was sought for non-payment at fines in Northamptonshire.

In respect of Ripon, to where Mrs M Lavin allegedly moved following leaving Haverfordwest coincidentally a Mr John Edward LAVIN resided at 9, Claremont, Ripon from 9 March

1943. The latter's previous address was recorded as being 40 Lawrence Street, Stockport.

Thus with all the co-incidences it is highly probable that the reporter for the missing person was Mrs Mary LAVIN, the wife of Jack (John Edward) LAVIN, despite denials by him of any knowledge and links to the 56 Stanley Street address. There is nothing on the file to indicate that Mary LAVIN was interviewed and challenged about these issues.

The reasons for the denial and the report being made remain unclear, however it is probable that it was personal gain, and that the alleged missing person CURLEY aka O'Grady was a fictitious individual.

There are on file a number of communications which, it would seem prudent not to follow as the basis for the content is at best questionable.

Suspects

During 1953, his former wife, UNA HAINSWORTH, identified JACK MOSSOP as a potential suspect following a submission. MOSSOP, in later life was suffering from mental illness and died in a mental institution in 1942. In 1932 the elationship of MOSSOP and the now HAINSWORTH produced a son, Julian MOSSOP, who remained with his mother unit 1949, when he went to London and there became involved in criminality. At the time of the discovery of the deceased, Julian MOSSOP was eleven years of age, living in Kenilworth and as such can be discounted as a suspect

Mrs HAINSWORTH seemingly had some history, as it would appear that the removal from the Kenilworth address left behind considerable debts.

Following their divorce and in the later part of his life Hainsworth and Mossop met where he alleged he was losing his mind, suffering from mental images of a woman in a tree leering at him. At this stage Hainsworth was obviously not aware of the Hagley body as it was yet to be discovered, and thought it was a delaying tactic for resolving issues.

114

With the discovery of the body and subsequent media attention in a pictorial, Hainsworth wrote a letter signing it 'Anna'. At that stage some assertions with regard to witchcraft had been made and she wished not to be associated with it.

The story she outlined was that a Dutch male called Van Ralt (term also includes the spelling Van Raalt hereafter) came to her home in 1940. He was seemingly without regular employment albeit he had considerable funds. Hainsworth made an aside that Van Ralt may have been a spy. This aside seems to be the basis for later conjecture that the death involved spies.

In March or April 1941, MOSSOP arrived home noticeably having had drank alcohol, and in an agitated state when he allegedly stated that he had been to the Lyttleton Arms with Van RALT and the 'Dutch piece' (Presumably this meant a female either Dutch in nationality or associated with the Dutchman Van RALT). MOSSOP allegedly stated that the female had become awkward then passed out. Van RALT directed MOSSOP to drive to a nearby wood where the former stuck her into a hollow tree and left her there. It was allegedly stated that she would come to her senses the following day and the men returned to Kenilworth.

There was and still remains a public house in Hagley called the Lyttleton Arms, which was located on the main Kidderminster to Birmingham Road. More latterly with road enhancements, the public house now sits on a side road.

The logical route back towards Kenilworth from the public house would have been through Clent, to Bromsgrove, and thence into Warwickshire. This route is the opposite direction to the wooded area on the main Birmingham Road where the deceased was recovered.

It would appear that there was a link between Van RALT and an act appearing at the Coventry Hippodrome in 1938, the performers being known as 'Frick and Frack' however the grounds for such a link is undefined.

Checks of the nationality database subsequent to 1948 (probably in 1953 following the disclosure by Mrs HAINSWORTH) identify two Van RALT nominals.

The first is Pieter Van RAALT who landed in 1948, and had an address in London SE25, the second was a female who held a permanent address in London but occupied a teaching position in Nottingham. Significantly, the female, Laura Frances Ryllis Van RAALTE had on 17th August 1940, vacationed in Malvern staying at the Beauchamp Hotel, and thus has arguably some relationship with Worcestershire.

There is nothing on the file to indicate whether it was possible in 1954 to establish whether Ms Van RAALTE was still alive, however there is a report concerning the individual using the present tense which would seem to indicate that in 1954 she was still surviving. If one is to take the post mortem report of Professor WEBSTER as being precise, then in 1940, Ms Van RAALTE was over forty years of age and would just about fall outside the requisite parameters for the deceased.

Lines of Enquiry
Nomination of Suspects
Following the disclosure by Hainsworth, Jack Mossop and Van Raalte appear to be worthy of review. If taken at face value, there are a number of factors, which would key in with the information known. Unfortunately it is now extremely difficult to clearly identify the degree of information which was released into the public arena which would allow for the story to be sewn together by Hainsworth.

In relation to the area of Hagley, Hainsworth may have had a degree of knowledge. When making the disclosure she was resident in Claverly, a small Shropshire village lying just outside the Wolverhampton conurbation. Hagley in those days would lie on a route between the Warwick, Shrewley areas and Claverly. It would appear that the Public House was quite well-known and was a point to where persons would travel for a day out. It was a waypoint in the general area of Hagley and Stourbridge used as a means of direction or a marker for directions.

Review of Status of Crime

The status of the crime as an unsolved murder is based considerably on the post-modern report of Professor Webster, in his field, Professor Webster was regarded as being pre-eminent, however with the passage of time, the Identification of new concepts, and the modification of previously held beliefs may result in a differing perspective being placed upon the cause of death. Exploration of this concept has been undertaken and there is no advantage taking this forward.

Witnesses

Whilst the only identified witnesses survive, these individuals can only proffer information surrounding the discovery of the remains, some substantial time following the death. Over the passage of time no other witnesses have been identified despite the factor that the death was broadcast nationally in an investigative style programme by John Stalker. The prospect of locating witnesses at this juncture is remote.

Media Appeals/ Communications Strategy

The prospect of receiving information, which would move the enquiry forward following a general media appeal, is minimal. Indeed the prospect is that the appeal would generate considerable interest from the perspective of obsessionalist, theorists and individuals as archived in the rear of the folder. The opportunity of working with an investigative journalist who seeks to undertake a programme or a part programme concerning the case is rather more appealing. This would potentially facilitate a mechanism of re awakening the public awareness, and those having genuine knowledge prompted to be in touch. That said, the case was subject to a television programme produced by John Stalker, broadcast nationally, which resulted in no additional material being forthcoming.

Arrest Strategy

The passage of time, the demise of MOSSOP and the hitherto non-identification of Van Raalte who would now be in the latter phase of this life, if indeed he has not predeceased this report. At this time there are no other potential offenders identified, thus an arrest is not envisaged.

Search Strategy

The passage of time has rendered impractical a search otherwise than in the event of the identification of a potential offender. It is highly likely that even after the passage of time, that the offender would maintain either media reporting or similar, and thus would be the subject of the search.

Interview Strategy

The interview strategy at this stage cannot be defined, but in the unlikely event of a suspect coming to notice this would be developed.

Identification Strategy

Identification of the deceased after this passage of time is somewhat difficult. There may well be opportunities to be explored in respect of DNA profiling and thereby gain a lineage match. Extensive enquiries to identify the resting-place of the remains have thus far failed.

An interment would have taken place, however it is unclear as to where the remains would be buried, and where the ownership of the remains lies.

Forensic Strategy

Consideration has been afforded to the use of the expertise of a Forensic Archaeologist, Forensic Anthropologist, Forensic Environmentalist, Palaeontologist and an Odentologist. Additionally the advances In DNA techniques have been researched

The Forensic Archaeologist may have been able to assist had there been any photographs of the scone recorded. At this stage I am unable to identify whether this was the case. Most certainly there is no record of such on the file. The scene has decayed over the passage of time as indeed has the tree, and thus no scene worthy of calling such remains.

The identification of the deceased has a potential to move the enquiry forward. This can potentially be achieved by virtue of DNA analysis of the remains, and extraction of the mitacondrial DNA. Furthermore the origins of the deceased could potentially be ascertained through analysis of the bone constituents thereby providing supportive structure to the assertions of Hainsworth.

The final resting-place of the bones has yet to be ascertained. In such cases, the remains were buried in a 'paupers' grave. Enquiries with the cemeteries within the Stourbridge and surrounding West Midlands's area have failed to identify the resting-place of the deceased. Thus without source material such forensic initiatives are flawed.

Conclusion

At this stage with the passage of time, there are no clear investigative leads. If the location of the remains were established, development of the DNA processes has not afforded investigative opportunities. Any person involved, if surviving, would be in excess of eighty years of age and the prospect of a prosecution would at best be remote.

I therefore make the following recommendations:
•The case is identified as being closed,
•Consideration should be afforded to placing the documentation in the Worcestershire Records Office as an historic document.

13 July 2005
I Nicholls
Detective Chief Inspector

MORE NON FICTION FROM APS PUBLICATIONS
(www.andrewsparke.com)

Aramoana (Andrew Sparke)
Beating The Banana: Breast Cancer and Me (Helen Pitt)
Bella In The Wych-Elm (Andrew Sparke)
Changing Lives: The Leaps and Bounds Method (Horsfall & Sparke)
Croc Curry & Texas Tea: Surviving Nigeria (Paul Dickinson)
Dub Poets In Their Own Words (Eric Doumerc)
Food and Cancer Prevention (Andrew Sparke)
Indie Publishing: The Journey Made Easy (Andrew Sparke)
Istanbul: The Visitor Essentials (Andrew Sparke)
More Swings Than Roundabouts: The Life of Carlos 'Robin' Medina (John Wright)
Piggery Jokery In Tonga (Andrew Sparke)
Rear Gunner(Andrew Sparke)
Stutthof (Andrew Sparke)
The Strange Free-Fall Of Fred Ryland (Helen Pitt)
The Ways Of Mevagissey (Andrew Sparke)
Tithes & Offerings (Rebirtha Hart)
War Shadows (Andrew Sparke)
What I Think About When I Think About Aikidoo (Mark Peckett)
Your Kid and Crohn's: A Parent's Handbook (William Sparke)

THE PHOTOGRAPHICS SERIES
Images (Andrew Sparke)
Istanbul In Pictures (Andrew Sparke)
Wild Life (David Kiteley)
Shapely Curves and Bumpers (Lee Benson)
Elsewhere (Joanna Leszczynska)

Made in the USA
Monee, IL
19 March 2022

93173883R00069